Praise for *Another Life*

"I have always believed that the greatest comeback story ever told is the story of redemption—and Darryl Strawberry's life is one of the most powerful examples of that I have ever seen.

In *Another Life*, Darryl pulls back the curtain on the pain, the failures, and the long road back—and he does it with raw honesty and deep grace. This is not a book about a man cleaning himself up and getting his life together. This is a book about a man who was transformed by the power of Jesus Christ. There is a big difference.

If you have ever felt like your past has disqualified you from your future, you need to read this book. Darryl Strawberry is living proof that no one is too far gone, no wound is too deep, and it is never too late for God to write a brand new chapter in your life.

Another Life is more than a memoir—it is a message of hope. And that is a message our world desperately needs right now."

—Greg Laurie, pastor of Harvest Christian Fellowship and evangelist for Harvest Crusades

"I managed Straw on the field, but his greatest victories came off it. This book shows the courage it takes to confront your past and embrace a new life—a story that will inspire anyone seeking redemption."

—Joe Torre, Hall of Fame manager

"Darryl Strawberry has been a brother to me through the highest of highs on the world's biggest stages and the toughest moments off the field. To witness his transformation into a man of such profound faith and purpose is the greatest 'comeback' I have ever seen. He was a titan in the dugout, but the man he is today is my true inspiration. I'm proud to stand in his corner, just as he has always stood in mine."

—David Cone, five-time World Series champion

"There was always a goodness in Darryl Strawberry, but that goodness would frequently lose the battle with the demons. Now he has conquered them and he is not just satisfied with his own salvation but has made the redemptive journeys of others his mission. He has turned one life into *Another Life* and it has been so satisfying to witness his amazing journey. I've always been his friend, and I wear that title proudly."

—Michael Kay, voice of the New York Yankees on YES Network

"There are moments in life when you recognize that certain relationships are not accidental—they are providential. I believe with all my heart that God places people in our paths for a reason, and my friendship with Darryl Strawberry is one of those moments. Behind the home runs and the headlines is a man whose life has been transformed by the grace of God.

In *Another Life*, Darryl opens his heart and shares the powerful story of redemption, restoration, and the healing power of Christ. His journey reminds us that no life is too broken for God to restore and no past is too far gone for His grace to reach. Darryl's willingness to share both the victories and the struggles of his life will encourage countless people who are searching for hope and a new beginning.

I truly believe that the testimony God has given Darryl will lead far more people to Christ than he could ever imagine. This book is not just a story—it is a witness to the life-changing power of God's grace."

—Dr. Gabriel L. Swaggart, pastor at Family Worship Center and president of Jimmy Swaggart Bible College

Another Life

Also by Darryl Strawberry

Turn Your Season Around: How God Transforms Your Life

Straw: Finding My Way

Also by Jerome Preisler

Game Face: A Lifetime of Hard-Earned Lessons On and Off the Court
(Bernard King, coauthor)

Daniel's Music: One Family's Journey from Tragedy to Empowerment Through Faith, Medicine, and the Healing Power of Music

Another Life

Discovering the Healing Power of Purpose on My Long Journey from Player to Preacher

DARRYL STRAWBERRY

with Jerome Preisler

BENBELLA

BenBella Books, Inc.

Dallas, TX

BenBella
8080 N. Central Expressway
Suite 1700
Dallas, TX 75206
benbellabooks.com
Send feedback to feedback@benbellabooks.com

Printed in the United States of America
10 9 8 7 6 5 4 3 2 1

Library of Congress Control Number: 2026007830
ISBN 9781637748848 (hardcover)
ISBN 9781637748855 (electronic)

Editing by Rick Chillot
Copyediting by Michael Fedison
Proofreading by Marissa Wold Uhrina
Text design and composition by Aaron Edmiston
Cover design by Morgan Carr
Cover phototography by Phil Cantor
Printed by Lake Book Manufacturing

This book is for my beloved wife, Tracy—the strongest, bravest, truest person I've ever met.

Just after the manuscript was delivered to our publisher, Tracy had to undergo major back-to-back surgeries. I was on the road ministering when she was ordered into the hospital for the second surgery. And what did she do after having that operation? Set up a Facetime with me and ask if I was okay! And by the way, was I alone in my travels or was my son Jordan there to look after me?

That's Tracy for you. Thoughtful, caring, and selfless even in her time of crisis, rock solid in her faith and love of family and friends, always generous to those in need.

Trace, you believed in me when no one else did. When I was lost in darkness, you took my hand, refused to let go, and guided me toward the Light and another life.

I wouldn't be who I am today without you. You're the ultimate overcomer and keeper of my heart.

Forever,
Darryl

Contents

Introduction

The Number of My Days

On March 11, 2024, right before my sixty-second birthday, I suffered a near-fatal heart attack. I know the reason I'm here today—alive, and able to have written this book—is that God still has work for me to do.

I'd been on the road for a week as a traveling minister and felt the warning signs. They first came on while I was hustling between airports and hotels to address a large group of athletes in Indiana. I tried to ignore the symptoms when they struck, though they were serious and kept getting worse.

Of course, I'm a former ballplayer. I may have "taken off my uniform" (a phrase you'll hear me use again) to surrender myself to God twenty years before, but athletes need a ton of stubbornness to succeed—and I was pretty hardheaded.

In competitive sports, especially a physical grind like Major League Baseball, you aren't just going up against the players in the other dugout. You're contending with pain, day in and day out, six or seven months a year. You're always dealing with nagging injuries, and there's never a time when some part of your body doesn't hurt. But once you step on the field, you push that pain aside.

You have to overcome it to stay out there and perform.

In my life as a preacher, I travel around the United States 270 days a year counseling people and delivering the Gospel. I'm usually accompanied by my son or my dear friend and fellow minister John Luppo. One day we might be in Tulsa, Oklahoma, the next in Albuquerque, New Mexico. Then New York, Louisiana, or anywhere else in the country.

It's rough being separated from my incredible wife, Tracy, for weeks at a time, but having Jordan and John with me is a true blessing. In these pages I'll share how my father–son relationship with Jordan has blossomed across the countless miles we've spent on the road.

Our travels together have bonded and changed us, and I believe parents—and anyone with young people in their lives—will be able to relate to our story. I hope some of you find inspiration in it.

But back to the heart attack. I had a full calendar of engagements that March, and the next month, and the next. Then, on June 1, the New York Mets were planning to retire my jersey number, 18, with a huge ceremony at a packed Citi Field.

For a former athlete, that's the honor of a lifetime. For someone who played under the Big Apple's bright lights, it's even more special. I was totally humbled. I could hardly wait to thank the organization and everyone who helped, encouraged, or just put up with me along the way: friends, family, and especially Tracy and my late mother, Ruby. More than anything, I wanted a chance to express my gratitude to all of them.

Finally, I had something I wanted to tell my fans, the Mets faithful. It was a truth I'd carried inside me for decades—and that they'd waited too long to hear.

With so much happening, the old-school ballplayer in me wouldn't slow down. I'd lost sixteen inches of intestine to colon cancer in 1998. In

2000, a tumor near my left kidney led to its removal. I'd battled addiction that nearly killed me, done a year in jail, and been divorced twice.

After all that, what were a few chest pains?

When Tracy sped me to SSM Health St. Joseph Hospital in St. Louis, I was in bad shape. I had a critical blockage in my aorta, and my heart was straining to function. Not much blood was getting through.

The heart attack nearly killed me—my doctors say it's a miracle I survived. I had a stent inserted, wore a defibrillator for weeks, and still take medication daily.

These days I feel great and am back to doing my work on behalf of the Lord. But if there's one thing I learned from overcoming my addictions, it's that recovery's an ongoing process. It always involves growth and change. And it always offers lessons in how to become better—physically, mentally, and spiritually. In the coming pages, you'll hear me talk a lot about how all three areas of our lives fit together.

I left the hospital with a deeper understanding that we're on this earth for a limited time. We never know when our time will come, and that obliges us to invest our best self in every moment. I'd been renewed and reenergized by a challenge I never expected. It was a powerful epiphany.

Now I tell people, "We only get one shot at this life—and we need to make it count."

That message is the main reason I wrote this book. But it isn't the only one.

In my *New York Times* bestselling memoir, *Straw: Finding My Way*, I gave an honest account of my baseball career and personal struggles. *Another Life* picks up where that book left off, bringing you into the most important chapter of my life—the reason I believe God put me here.

I'm going to write about it with that same honesty. You may agree or disagree with something I say, but you'll always know I'm being real.

I believe you can receive grace, but you need to give it back. A lot of people are suffering inside, trying to get free of their pain. And two of the most important life lessons I've learned from fame, failure, cancer, drug addiction, prison, brokenness, recovery—and most recently the heart attack—are that we all need to examine what we want to do with our time on earth, and that we all have something to give back and help somebody else.

In *Another Life*, I talk a lot about the work I'm doing at the "back end," because I believe life's later innings are about paying forward what we learn through experience—about extending to others the grace and healing we've received.

When I take us back to my darker periods, it's only to put things in perspective. Once we understand the past, we can make the most of the present—and prepare to shape the future.

Notice I don't say *my present* or *my future*. The Bible is a simple book for complicated people—and that means every single one of us. Its stories and parables hold rich moral and spiritual lessons to guide us through life's trials. While I'm sure not comparing anything I write to Scripture, I believe the Word is a strong model to follow.

It's never too late to restore and transform ourselves. Wherever we are, no matter our circumstances, they're never our true destination. The real journey's always in our hearts, minds, and souls. Can we control what the world throws at us? We only wish. But we can control how we face each moment. We can choose the kind of person we want to be.

Would you rather be whole and free to be happy—or broken and traumatized by the past? I'm guessing most of us would shout out a loud, clear YES! to the first part of my question.

But how do we get there? Where does the journey even start?

Inner pain is at the root of our emotional problems. If we don't face our pain and deal with it both spiritually and emotionally, we all become its prisoners.

And that's only half of it. The real value of the lessons that free us from pain—their whole purpose—is to use them to help free someone else.

Wherever I travel, my role as minister stays the same: to bring hope by sharing how good God is and to show through my own experiences that He's a forgiving and merciful God.

I see fractured, hurting, lost, and lonely people everywhere. And I have a responsibility to tell them, "You're not alone. We all have struggles. But we don't have to stay stuck in them. We can't quit on ourselves. We pick ourselves up, go forward, and find peace."

One of the most enjoyable and rewarding parts of writing this book has been the chance to introduce you to many great community leaders I've met while traveling the country—people and organizations working to build a brighter world.

Business professionals, students, survivors of addiction and abuse, everyday men and women . . . we can all experience inner growth and spiritual transformation. We can all improve. And we can all help make things better for the rest of us.

As you'll see, I dedicate a full chapter to a visit Tracy and I made to America's largest maximum-security penitentiary, Angola Prison, where we shared God's message of healing with hundreds of inmates.

I'm blessed that the Lord has given me the opportunity to travel to prisons around the country. When I tell people about that part of my calling, they often say it sounds like something they would find oppressive and hard to get through. But I always reply that it's one of my greatest joys.

I find preaching to inmates gratifying, uplifting, and downright remarkable. It's important to shine a compassionate light on these outsiders—people who've been marginalized and forgotten by society and, in some cases, by their own choices.

Have they made serious mistakes? Hurt far too many innocent victims? The answer is that they have, and it's tragic—especially for those victims and their loved ones. But I also know God doesn't make mistakes, and we're all His creations. I've met men who've been behind bars for fifty years. Many will spend the rest of their lives behind concrete walls and razor wire. But they're as human as anyone else.

It's no secret that I had an abusive father, and that my brother and I once considered killing him to protect our mother and ourselves. If we'd gone through with that plan, I might have spent a big chunk of my life behind bars—and it's a safe bet my baseball career wouldn't have happened. I knew kids in our South Central Los Angeles neighborhood who were placed in juvenile detention and then spiraled into even worse situations. Who knows what destructive paths I might have taken?

Even after the World Series championships and All-Star appearances, my poor decisions led to my serving eleven months in a Florida jail from 2002 to 2003.

I never forgot the lessons I learned.

Twenty years later, I'd occasionally drive past Northern State Prison heading to the Newark, New Jersey, airport and feel compelled to deliver my message to the men inside. When I finally went to address a group of prisoners there, the turnout brought tears to my eyes. It was the first of many prison visits—I fit at least two a year into my schedule these days.

For me, the work of ministering never stops. Do I get tired? Physically, yes. Aching airplane-seat knees, hotel-mattress back—they go with the territory. But I love and cherish every minute of it. My heart attack made me see more clearly than ever how temporary life is. Eventually, our clocks run out. But there's power in purpose. It recharges me and keeps me showing up, because I know I'm helping change lives.

In the pages that follow, I'll use my personal story of recovery, redemption, and restoration to illustrate how we all can have richer, happier, more joyous days by coming to terms with what's broken and hurting inside us.

My hope is that you'll find encouragement, enlightenment, and maybe a few smiles in these pages to accompany your own journeys.

And so, I want to thank you for picking up this book. I didn't expect to be writing another one, and wouldn't have unless I felt it would offer something unique—and positive—you can apply to your own experience. By walking in this world with principles and values, we can share what we learn through example, lighting the path forward with compassion and generosity.

In that way, we can all reach a place of greater physical, emotional, and spiritual health together.

Chapter One

Living Right

"You're going to go through it. But He's going to get it out of you."

It was February 1996, a couple of months before the start of my second season with the New York Yankees. My mother, Ruby, was dying from breast cancer, and I was at her bedside.

Moments before saying those words, she'd asked me to pray for her.

My life was falling apart. I had wealth, great fame, and was tearing through a crazy fast-lane lifestyle. On the outside, I seemed to have everything. But none of it made me happy. For me, happiness meant having more of everything.

I would learn the hard way that I was wrong—dead wrong—but that was still years in the future. A sinner in need of a Savior, I did not know Mama was praying for me behind the scenes.

And now she wanted me to pray for *her*. I wasn't sure I knew the right words. But Mama always knew better. She was always my greatest intercessor.

I gave her a look. It was like she was warning about a Category 5 hurricane tracking straight for me. I had been married and divorced, fought multiple addictions, earned and lost millions, and made a total wreck of my life. I'd struggled to save my Major League career—all in the public spotlight. *Go through what?*

"Mama, don't tell me that," I said. "I need a drink."

She didn't bat an eye. "You go right ahead and get one," she said in her calm, quiet voice. "After you pray."

I sat there a second. She held her eyes steady on mine.

"Don't forget," she said. "He's going to get it out of you."

I bowed my head and did my best. When I finished, Mama looked at peace.

She passed away a few weeks later, our whole family gathered around her. My brother Ron was going through his own trials at the time, and it took us a while to track him down. But she hung on until he was at her side. I'll always be convinced she willed it with God's help.

As for me: My mother's words eventually came true, though it would be a long while before they sank in. She didn't need to spell things out. Ruby Strawberry rarely raised her voice and never laid a hand on any of her five children. She taught us by example, how she carried herself through good and bad times.

Make your life count with your actions. That was her unspoken message. Whatever you go through—both the highs and lows—just make them count. For her, that meant doing good in this world, extending kindness and compassion to others, and passing on what we learn from experience. A woman of steady but understated Baptist faith, Ruby lived by the Bible's fundamental principles. She knew in her heart it was a simple guide through a complicated life.

Mama's life was filled with challenges. The greatest might have been her dysfunctional marriage to my father, Henry—but she never let their broken relationship break *her*.

Henry Strawberry was an alcoholic, a compulsive gambler, and a violent and psychologically abusive man. They called him Big Hank around the ballpark because of his physical stature, which I inherited (I'm 6'6"). And his size wasn't the only thing he passed on. He was a great athlete too.

Dad worked for the postal service and played on its softball team, the Wildcats. He could flat-out throw and swing a bat—blowing guys away with his fastball and mashing the ball hard enough to drive it past most outfielders. It made him close to a legend in his league. But when he wasn't in bars after games, or at the horse track, he was coming home in a surly mood.

Of the five kids, Ronnie and I were his whupping posts. He'd lay us across the bed with our shirts off and tower over us, holding an electrical extension cord from the vacuum cleaner. He might have thought he was disciplining us, but we never knew what for.

I doubt he really knew either. Abuse is never rational.

Dad would beat us and say, "You're never going to be nothing. You don't do nothing right." It was just so bad. I can still hear his voice, see the welts on my brother's back. Worse than the beatings, I was terrified deep inside that what he was telling me was true. At my core, I came to believe I was worthless. That I'd never amount to anything in this world.

One night when he came home drunk, Dad got rough with my mom. I was thirteen, and Ronnie a year older, the two of us still sharing a bedroom. We heard him yelling at her through the door. My older brother Mike was home, and he finally confronted Dad on the other side of that door, told him to get out of there and leave us alone.

That only threw him into a worse rage. He pulled a shotgun out of the closet and started waving it around and making threats.

"I'll kill all y'all!" he hollered.

But Ron and I had come up with a plan even before he got home. We'd decided we weren't going to let him beat us or Mama anymore. The next time he raised a hand to her would be the last time he'd hurt any of us.

As we left our room and hurried toward the dining room, dad was following Mike around the table in a circle, like he was going to do something awful to him. That was when Ronnie grabbed a butcher knife, and I took hold of a frying pan. Ronnie was thinking along the same lines as me: *The only one dying here tonight is Dad.*

There was more shouting. As my father finally started to back down, my mom was screaming at us to get out of the house and go down to a neighbor's place, where we could be safe. The racket coming from our windows was loud enough to be heard up and down the block.

Henry never set foot through the door again, leaving my mother to raise five kids on her own.

It would have been easy for her to become jaded and embittered. Bringing us up as a single mother after their split brought a new set of struggles. But she never complained.

Mom was our anchor. We didn't have a strong male figure around the house. There was no encouraging father's voice to say, "You can do it. You're good enough, you're smart enough." Even when he was around, Henry's message was always that we were good for nothing.

But in one way, the Strawberry kids couldn't have been luckier. We got the opposite from Mama—a sweet, hardworking woman of faith who led by example.

Born in the 1940s, Ruby belonged to what I call the Get-Up-and-Go generation. Get up to take care of your family. Go to work. Even if it's hard, never give up. Don't quit. Pursue the right way of living. She started out as a secretary at Pacific Bell and eventually became a circuit designer—a big step up for a woman of color at the time.

These were both coveted jobs, and Mama holding them for so many years was a testament to her work ethic and commitment to her children.

Ruby Strawberry never for a moment felt sorry for herself, and she refused to let us feel that way about ourselves—again, setting an example. Being Black and from South Central Los Angeles, one of the poorest, toughest neighborhoods in America, it would have been easy to believe our father, and think we'd never make it out or succeed at anything. He'd shattered our self-esteem, and we saw despair all around us on the street.

Mama wouldn't let that negativity into our home after he left. She felt responsible for giving us hope and wanted us to see her as a beacon. Despite her struggling to support our family as a single mother—in those days, women didn't earn anything close to men's salaries—she refused to ever allow our circumstances to be an excuse for quitting. Her focus was not on what we couldn't afford but on appreciating what we had. On counting our blessings.

Did she have the means to give us everything we wanted? No. But she made sure we got what we needed. She kept a roof over our heads, put three meals a day on the table, and always found the money for our clothes and school supplies. When she saw how much I wanted to play baseball, she managed to save enough out of her paycheck to buy a glove and cleats. Looking back, I see that determination and sacrifice as incredible.

Mama didn't have much left over for herself after spending what she brought home on her children. But I can't recall her ever treating us as a drain or hindrance. She considered all five of us gifts from God—that's truly how she saw it. When she became ill with cancer, and then realized the disease would take her life, she took comfort in knowing she'd already raised us and given us solid ground to stand on.

She didn't leave a legacy of broken promises. Hers was doing all she could to be sure her children would stand up and live right. I think she'd have seen it as a gift for a gift.

For Mama, living right meant being loving, giving, and caring toward others. She wanted us to see the good in people—a good everyone can grow within themselves and share. I often say that pursuing life is about navigating its storms with grace. That's what my mother showed us while going through all her personal storms.

Not long after Mama died, my sister found a journal under her mattress. Ruby knew each one of her children well, and understood the different challenges we still had to overcome. The journal held her wishes and prayers for all of us—me, Ronnie and Michael, and my younger sisters, Regina and Michelle. In many ways, it held the key to our futures.

The story of my learning to live a life of giving—and more importantly, my understanding of what it means to pay our blessings forward, passing them on to future generations—began with my mother. I still take great strength from her example. Much of her wisdom took time to sink in. But it's at the root of the man I eventually became.

Mama was never impressed by my fame as a ballplayer. She was proud of my accomplishments, but she also knew about the nonstop partying, drugs, and womanizing. And she prayed in her journal that God would knock me off my throne—that He would humble and save me.

With my wife Tracy's help, He did. And while I take great pride in what I accomplished on the field, I've come to see that I'm nothing without Christ's love and grace.

Everyone has to overcome something. We all face obstacles. But we can all still do something every day to leave the world a little better. If we make a positive difference in just one person's life, it lifts us all up higher.

Tracy and I have faced our own struggles, together and apart. We've walked down some dark roads and taken the journey of being redeemed and restored. When we established Strawberry Ministries, our goal was to bring what we learned to others in need of healing.

We've received tremendous grace in our lives. Paying it forward is how we show our appreciation.

We believe the best example we can set is a living one, and never wanted to preach our faith without living it. Though we always knew the ministry could be a game changer for others, we couldn't have guessed how much our work would help us grow as people, giving us a fresh look at what restoration really means.

Which brings me back full circle to my mother, Ruby, and the light she sheds over me to this day, so many years after she moved on. As I write these words, I can almost see her looking at me from her bed, and hear her low but firm voice:

You're going to go through it, but He's going to get it out of you.

I'll never be sure whether that was her wish, a premonition, or a little of both. But I do know it would be selfish of me to receive the healing forgiveness of God's love without passing it on to as many people as I can.

In my mom's spirit, let's celebrate lives of giving to others. Let's be lights for those around us.

Trust me when I say doing that is more satisfying than hitting a three-run homer—though I won't kid you, that's about as fun as it gets!

Chapter Two

Lord, You Really Are Testing Me

If you want to take me Home, I'm good with it. If you want to leave me here on earth to finish my work, I'm okay with it too.

But PLEASE don't let me die before my big day!

I'm going over my contract with God Almighty, while being wheeled into the O/R on a hospital gurney—and hoping He's a good sport about granting that one request. A moment ago, I saw my wife, Tracy, walk off down a separate hallway toward the waiting room.

We can only hope and pray we'll see each other again in this world.

It's Monday evening, March 11, 2024, a day before my sixty-second birthday, and we're at St. Joseph Hospital West, a few miles from where I live in St. Louis. The doctors rushing me into emergency lifesaving surgery say I was in grave condition when I arrived.

I should have seen it coming. But I didn't.

I was on the road all week, crisscrossing the country on behalf of Strawberry Ministries, the organization my wife, Tracy, and I cofounded to help people recover from mental, emotional, and spiritual pain and find better lives through the power of Christ.

Five days earlier, I'd left home for a speaking engagement in Fort Wayne, flying from Lambert International Airport to Atlanta's Hartsfield-Jackson, where I was supposed to make a connection to Indiana. My son Jordan travels with me whenever we can synch our schedules, and for that particular road trip he flew on ahead to Atlanta, planning to meet me there during his layover so we could fly on together. But naturally, my plane arrived late. You can always count on that happening when you're in a hurry.

My heart was racing as I rushed to the departure gate, firing off text messages to Jordan so he'd know I would try my best to make our flight . . . and that was when I suddenly felt I had to slow down.

Bear in mind, that's not me. In my long career as a ballplayer, I was used to playing through all kinds of physical pain. But this was different. My head was spinning. My legs felt like jelly. I was afraid they'd just give out, and that I'd collapse to the floor of the crowded airline terminal, with hundreds of people around me hustling toward their destinations.

Pull back, I thought. *Slow down.*

As I slowed my pace, I could feel my heart slowing inside me, and I figured I'd be all right. But I was shaken up. The dizziness and weakness, the runaway heartbeat. I'd never experienced anything like it before. Not in my whole life.

By that time, I'd missed my flight and knew I would have to arrange for a new connection. With a long wait ahead, I took the escalator up to The Club—a big lounge area on the airport's mezzanine—and called Tracy. I needed to tell her what I'd experienced.

"This doesn't sound good," she said before I could finish. "I think you should see a doctor."

I always say Tracy takes better care of me than I do, and I knew deep down I ought to pay attention. But I didn't want to make a big deal out of things. The stubborn athlete in me again. Play through pain.

"Nah, I'll be all right," I said. "I'll take it easy and grab something to eat."

Getting some food into my stomach helped. When I reached Fort Wayne later on, I met Jordan and rested up in our hotel room. All things considered, I felt okay. But I was still fatigued, and Jordan was watching me like a hawk. Tracy had phoned ahead to alert him about my episode in Atlanta, and since he'd played college ball—and a few years pro in Russia and Europe—he listened to the coach and covered his man. We'd been having a lot of talks lately about life, faith, and about being fathers, so I didn't really notice he was tuned in more than usual.

That night we went out to dinner, then drove straight back to the hotel to turn in early. The next evening I'd be the keynote speaker at a benefit supporting the Fellowship of Christian Athletes, and I wanted to feel rested and ready to rock.

The event had a strong turnout and couldn't have gone better. But when I stepped to the podium my heart started to race again, just like at the airport. It kept pounding the whole time I spoke, and this time I also felt a burning sensation in my chest.

I tried to brush it off. When I'm on the road, I tend to eat later than usual. The night before, I did exactly that. So, I told myself it was just some mild indigestion. But deep down I knew something was very wrong.

After the banquet, Jordan and I drove our rented Suburban to Indianapolis, a straight shot down I-69. The plan was to sleep over in a hotel near the airport, and then take an early flight to New York for a Sunday appearance.

I started out behind the wheel, but within an hour I got so tired that I turned the driving over to Jordan. This also fit the that's-not-me category. If you know me, you know I'm *always* the driver. Everybody else hops in for the ride.

In New York, I stayed at a friend's house and still wasn't feeling too well. But I chalked it up to being a little worn out, and decided I just needed a break from my crammed schedule. As soon as I had a chance, I'd take one, I told myself.

There was nothing on the agenda for Friday and Saturday, giving me a chance to sleep late and relax. On Sunday morning, I did a charity event. It was great, but I felt drained again afterward.

I'd done my Kingdom work. The long trip was almost over. I'd catch some rest when I was back home.

That afternoon, I headed over to LaGuardia Airport in Queens—right next door to Citi Field, where the Mets play their home games—for the flight back to St. Louis.

LaGuardia used to be one of the most cramped and overcrowded major airports in the country. But its recent renovation changed all that. Nowadays it's really spread out, so it was a long way from the terminal entrance to the gates.

As I walked through the concourse, I started feeling strange again. My heart was beating even faster than in Atlanta. My strength was gone, and I was sweating like I was pushing a cart of bricks uphill. I remember buying some water and emptying the bottle with big, deep gulps.

As it turned out, my gate was way at the end of the departure area. *Lord, You are really testing me*, I thought. *Making sure I can push through . . . whatever it is I'm going through.*

I slept for the entire flight back to St. Louis. As soon as I got home, I climbed into bed and snoozed late into Monday morning. Meanwhile, Tracy had gone into the office at Journey Church in Troy, a town not far from us, for some meetings.

A little past noon, she came home to pick me up for lunch. By then I was awake and feeling all right. Not great, and still drained, but all right.

That wouldn't last. We were out at a restaurant having sushi when my chest clamped up. I don't know how else to describe it, but I could tell Tracy noticed.

"What's wrong?" she asked. She looked worried.

"I don't know," I said. It was the truth. But I was running out of reasons to ignore whatever was going on with me.

We left the restaurant and came home. I was all out of gas, and still felt that tightness in my ribs. That iron clamp around my heart.

I could see Tracy was finished with my excuses.

"Okay, this is it," she said. "You look terrible. We're going to the hospital."

Except I didn't want to go. It was the old baseball player inside me. Athletes are used to pain. The best players from my generation took it as just another challenge built into the game, like batting against an ace pitcher, running the base paths, or diving for a fly ball in the outfield. To be great, you must handle pain. If you're injured, you play through it. If it means you have to hobble up to the plate, you wrap your leg with tape and hobble. Pain's an obstacle to overcome. The more pain we feel, the more we want to beat it and keep going. To stay on the field.

And so, the more Tracy tried to rush me, the more I stalled.

"I need to use the bathroom and do Number Two," I said, not realizing how crazy that sounded until I saw the look on her face. *Number Two?*

"You're kidding me, right?"

I shook my head. "That's first. Then I want to shower."

She gave me the fearsome wife squinch. I was in trouble. "Any more excuses?"

"No," I said, still hoping whatever was wrong with me would pass. "Then we go."

She wasn't happy. But I did both, knowing it was only postponing the inevitable. Tracy was determined. And when she's in that state of mind, there's no fighting her.

Once she finally hustled me into the car, she drove to St. Joseph West at warp speed.

"Tracy, relax," I insisted. "I'll be all right. This isn't an emergency."

She ignored my nonsense and zoomed along, her eyes locked on the road. "You need to get there," she said.

Her tone made it clear who was in charge.

Hint—it wasn't me.

When we reached the hospital, Tracy pushed out the driver's door and went into action, giving the doctors and nurses the rundown about my symptoms. In minutes they were drawing my blood, taking chest X-rays, hooking me up to EKG machines . . . running a full battery of tests.

The results showed I was in trouble.

"We have to get you some help right away," the doctor said. Later, he'd tell us he was amazed I'd gone all those days without critical care and survived.

So much for it not being an emergency. I was not only having a serious cardiac event, but my heart had been losing function for five days.

By the time I stepped into the ER, I was in grave condition.

And now I'm being wheeled into surgery, the gurney's wheels making a loud racket in the corridor.

Thankfully, the doctors say I have a few things going for me. Overall, I'm in good physical shape—that helped tip the scales in my favor for surviving colorectal cancer in 1998 when I was playing for the Yankees. Two years later, it was a huge factor in my recovery from a second cancer operation.

But I haven't always been careful about my health in the years since. My weight's been up and down. Not too long ago, I noticed I'd put on a few too many pounds. My clothes felt tight, and I would lose my breath doing easy workouts, or even bending to pick something up. When that happened, I improved my eating habits and started taking better care of my body.

I've got a cranky shoulder from crashing into a wall to make a play at Dodger Stadium—and I have the knees of a 6'6" outfielder who used to lope, sprint, and dive after every deep fly ball. But the parts have held together pretty well.

Maybe that's why this feels so unreal.

Not once during my five-day trip did I imagine I'd wind up in the hospital. Even a few minutes ago, while being poked, jabbed, and scanned in the ER, I was still expecting to be released with a prescription and a doctor's orders to get some bed rest.

Yet here I am, stretched out on my back in a blue hospital johnny, staring up at the ceiling as I'm wheeled toward an operating room to have a lifesaving stent placed in my aorta.

It hits me like a lightning bolt: I'm not in control of my life. None of us is. We like to think we are, but we aren't. And I'm at the height of mine, traveling the country to preach God's Word.

A heart attack? *This can't be happening to me*, I think. Cannot. I have too much work to do.

My calendar's packed with visits—each representing hundreds of lives I hope to impact.

And then, of course, there's my Big Day—the one I remind God about from my stretcher. It's coming up fast, in just three months.

On June 1, the New York Mets are retiring my jersey number with a ceremony at Citi Field that'll be seen on live TV and covered in all the major newspapers, sports blogs, vlogs, and podcasts. The Mets announced it the year before and set the date back in January, so fans could pick up their tickets in advance. They expect a capacity crowd, along with invited guests.

In case you aren't a sports fan: This is a huge deal. A legacy day. There's no greater honor for a baseball player than a team retiring his number, meaning it's never again going to be issued to another player. Not in ten years, or a hundred.

The Mets are the team that drafted me when I was only eighteen years old. The team I played on when I was voted National League Rookie of the Year and became a seven-time All-Star. It's the team I won my first World Series with back in 1986—the second and most recent championship in its sixty-three-year history.

I want to stand on the field and acknowledge everybody who helped me succeed in New York—my family, childhood friends, and the coaches and teammates who taught me so much and fought alongside me. I look forward to thanking the Mets fans who supported me through thick and thin, and intend to tell them about a silent regret I've kept in my heart for years. I want to express my appreciation to so many people in and outside the game . . . and most of all, I want to thank the two women who never gave up on me: my mother, Ruby, for everything she did to raise me right, and Tracy for saving my life, leading me back to Christ, and helping me become the person I am today.

I want to share that moment of gratitude with so many, and pray I'll still get the chance. But I have to let go and trust in God and my medical team.

Nothing is clearer to me than that as I'm rushed into surgery, with a thousand thoughts racing through my mind.

Chapter Three

A Good and Perfect Gift

It's a hot, sunny June afternoon in Queens, three and a half months since the heart attack, and I'm sitting in the home dugout at Citi Field, dressed sharp in a medium blue suit and tie, soaking it all in.

My eyes roam from the crowded upper decks to the 17,400-square-foot jumbotron above the center field wall, where highlights from my career flash across the screen. In New York, baseball's serious business—the fans get far more worked up over postseason runs than political campaigns. Not many players know the heights I experienced playing in front of those fans, helping bring a World Series trophy home with what might be the greatest team in modern history. Over three decades after my last game with the Mets, my 252 home runs still hold the franchise record—as of this date.

There's nothing wrong with taking pride in our accomplishments. *Every good and perfect gift is from above.* That's James 1:17, and far be it from me to question an apostle. More than anything, though, I feel grateful—a deep, humbling, and profound kind of gratitude. It's like a wave flowing through me that's both worldly and spiritual.

As I look over the dugout rail, I know that everything I've lived through—every wound, every struggle, every blessing—has led to this unbelievable moment. I'm thankful to everyone who's come from near and far to share it with me, from the guests of honor seated on the infield grass to the fans in the upper levels of the park. Above all, I thank God for letting me be here to see the day.

The chairs are arranged in a V on either side of second base—or where the base pad normally sits. Right now it's been replaced by a podium that's just waiting there for me.

To its right are my kids: DJ, Diamond, Jordan, Jade, Jewel, Alice, Omar, Austin, Evan . . . and my wife, Tracy.

On the left side of the diamond, I see Steve Cohen and his wife, Alex, the Mets' owners. I see the team's current manager, Carlos Mendoza. And I see members of the '86 team—guys who inspired me to be better and with whom I won a championship: Ron Darling. John Franco. John Gibbons. Keith Hernandez—the most intense teammate ever. He drove me to be successful and taught me how to hit left-hand pitching. Doc Gooden. Howard Johnson—HoJo. We were the only 30/30 players in baseball history who did it together, on the same team. There's Barry Lyons, Kevin Mitchell, Jesse Orosco—The Anchor—and Rafael Santana.

One person who isn't on the field today is our great manager Davey Johnson. Davey's had a few health issues and couldn't make the trip from his home in Florida, but he's there in all our hearts. Without him, there's no '86 trophy. He's the greatest manager I ever played for.

I remember early on, after the '82 minor league season, I went to play winter ball in Venezuela. I was just twenty years old, facing off against a whole mix of guys—some who had been in the big leagues, some in Triple-A. It was a different kind of competition, and it really pushed me to another level. The guys I played with told me I was headed to the big leagues if I kept working hard and playing the way I was.

The next year, I started the season in Triple-A. I got off to a good start, but one day I showed up at the ballpark and wasn't in the lineup. I asked Davey what was up, and he told me to come into his office. Then he said, "I'm not playing you today because you're going to the big leagues tomorrow." That was a moment I'll never forget.

Another thing I'll always remember about Davey is that he was ahead of his time when it came to using stats. He took a college computer class back in the late sixties—while he was still playing—and built a program around batting numbers. But he combined all that with an old-school mind and made sure we all knew our roles.

I guess you could say Davey understood the numbers, but he also understood people. And that combination made him really special.

I could go on about Davey Johnson for hours. But I haven't even gotten to my family yet, and there are a lot of them in the park besides those on the field.

My father-in-law, Jerry, for instance. He's up in the stands waiting for the ceremony to get started—and he's wearing a Mets jersey.

That might not sound like much on the surface, but it deserves a little unpacking.

Tracy and I had been living in Miami for years when she called her parents back home in St. Louis, where they'd both been born and raised.

"I'm coming home from Florida," she said. "And I'm bringing Darryl Strawberry."

To put her announcement in its place: Once upon a time, the Mets and the St. Louis Cardinals were in a fierce division rivalry—and it only got more heated in 1983, when the Mets traded for Keith Hernandez, a favorite of Cards fans. By the time I came up to the Majors, Keith's intensity had rubbed off on the whole team. The toughest competitor I ever played with, he started the turnaround that made us champions.

In 1985, St. Louis edged us for the division by three games, going

101–61 to our second-place 98–64. Winning that many games and missing the postseason stuck in our throats. I remember we cried bitter tears in the locker room and swore we'd get them back the next season.

That doesn't always happen . . . but it did for us. We roared past St. Louis and the rest of the National League East with a 108-win season—one of the best records in MLB history. With most of our core group intact, we came back with purpose and fire, and we didn't let up until we were on top.

Naturally, Cardinals fans weren't exactly showering us with love. And as for the fan who happened to be my future father-in-law . . .

Midwestern dads aren't the type to say a lot. They're like old oaks, still and steady. When Tracy told him she was bringing me home, her father said—cue that Midwestern reserve:

"He played for the Mets."

And then he dropped the phone. *Clunk!*

And now, here's Jerry wearing a Mets jersey. Meanwhile, Howie Rose, the Mets radio announcer, is speaking at the podium, getting ready to bring me onto the field. And I'm standing there thinking . . .

Only a month ago, I could barely get out of bed without losing my breath. Everything about today—my whole future as a traveling minister—felt like it was hanging by a thread.

I've talked about the moment of clarity when I was being rolled into surgery—when it struck me I wasn't in control of my life. I'd always thought I was managing things, balancing my marriage and fatherhood with the busy, nonstop life of a traveling minister. But at that point, I realized I wasn't in control. I was completely in the care of my medical team, trusting God to guide their hands.

It felt unreal. My struggles with drugs and alcohol were long behind me. I'd been through serious health scares before, but they were also in the rearview mirror. I'm diabetic, but I stay on top of it, keeping my blood sugar levels stable through commonsense exercise, medication, and a good diet. As we get older, we need to maintain ourselves spiritually and physically. Our bodies still experience wear and tear. We all have stuff to deal with.

But a heart attack?

I couldn't believe it. Couldn't believe the timing. *As if that's something any of us can ever control.*

I was at the height of my life of service to the Lord—traveling the country, preaching, helping people. I was going to churches, youth homes, and prisons—maximum-security prisons, where inmates were behind bars for decades or doing life without parole. I had a whole slate of events coming up: fundraising banquets, charity appearances, important opportunities to make a difference.

A couple of weeks before Tracy raced me to the ER, I'd visited Boys Town, a home for juvenile offenders, where I talked to the kids about the challenges I encountered in my own young life. By sharing what I'd learned from overcoming my emotional and psychological wounds, I knew I could help them heal from theirs. It all brought me so much joy.

And then the rug got pulled out from under me.

Heart problems have been the hardest challenges I've ever faced when it comes to my health. When you have cardiovascular issues, everything changes. You're used to your body working normally, but when your heart isn't strong, it all falls apart.

There's something about the heart being at the center of your body—your core. Your mobility and breathing depend on it. But you don't think about this until it isn't working right. When my heart wasn't functioning properly, I couldn't get up on my feet, or stay up, on my own. That can be a lonely place, even knowing through my faith that none of us are ever truly alone. If I had my wish, no one else would have to face such vulnerability. But we're all flesh and blood, not machines. And even the best-made machines have parts that wear down.

The uniform retirement ceremony was a godsend during my

recovery, because it put a hard deadline before me, and gave me daily incentive to get out of bed and work on regaining my strength.

Of course I didn't know that when I first got the news. It was early in the winter when Steve Cohen and team VP Jay Horwitz (who'd been like a father to me since I came up to the Majors) called to say they were retiring my number. They said Doc Gooden's number would be retired in April and offered a date in either May or June.

I picked June because my May calendar was busy with ministerial work, and I felt I needed a little time to prepare. I had to make a guest list, call people who'd been important in my life, write my speech . . .

All that would take a while, so we set the date for June 1.

Then I hung up the phone and let the enormity of it sink in.

Cohen had purchased the team in 2020, and he brought many alumni back under the franchise's wing, recognizing our achievements. Guys like Doc and me never really felt valued by the previous ownership. We were the first two homegrown starting pieces in a run of success that began in 1984—my second year in the Majors and Doc's first. That run lasted six years and ended in 1990, when my relationship with the front office deteriorated, and I left in free agency.

For years, I didn't look back. The organization showed little interest in celebrating the team's history and our contributions. But here, a new owner had taken over—a fan who grew up in Great Neck, New York, the heart of Mets country. That changed things in a big way.

It was such an incredible honor. I truly felt I was receiving another gift from my Maker. Best of all, the invitation came when I was spiritually whole and ready to embrace that part of my life again.

I don't feel it's important that fans know what kind of commitment goes into becoming a great baseball player—no more than it is for anyone to know what goes into being great at any other profession. A lifetime of training and practice, the workouts, the countless hours in the training room getting your arms and legs wrapped and iced—none of it has to matter to a fan watching you play 162 games a year . . . and if you're lucky, a full postseason. They pay to enjoy your performance. Performing well is your end of the deal.

In the same way, people don't need to know the ins and outs of what it took to come back from my addictions and become a minister. What matters is knowing that it's *possible* to come back. That if I could reclaim my life, there's hope for everyone.

But for me, what made the acknowledgment I was about to receive so meaningful was that it didn't just celebrate my baseball career. It honored that I'd come through everything to become the man I was meant to be—the spiritual journey no one saw. And it honored Tracy, without whom I wouldn't have made the journey.

I first accepted Christ in 1991. I'd left the Mets and signed a $20 million contract to play with the Los Angeles Dodgers. That was a lot of money—then and now—and you'd think I would've been at the top of the world. But I wasn't. I was an alcoholic, a drug addict, and a womanizer. I was going through a divorce with my first wife. I felt broken.

One day, her uncle took me to a Morris Cerullo crusade in Anaheim. Everyone had heard of him from his books and TV show, so I was curious.

I spent four nights hearing him preach the Gospel, and I never stopped crying. On the last night, Sunday, I remember him saying, and these are his exact words: "Whoever is here that needs experience with the Lord, you can come down on your own. It's up to you."

So I came down to the stage, got in line, and he laid hands on me. And through him, I felt the power of God. I went down on my knees, weeping, and then a guy in the crowd pulled me up.

He said, "I don't know who you are, but the Lord's called you."

I smiled through my tears. I told him he reminded me of my mother, Ruby, who always said the Lord had a purpose for me.

But I didn't have a solid foundation at the time. I didn't receive mentorship or study the Scriptures like I should have—and without that education, I couldn't really grow.

Just a few weeks into that first season with LA, I crashed into the outfield wall and dislocated my shoulder. I'd been hurt before, but nothing ever kept me off the field that long. I was out for over a month and a half, and it killed me to be starting out that way with my hometown team. I fell back into my bad habits—drinking, drugging, women. And I was lost and broken for the next fifteen years, dropping in and out of recovery, constantly in legal trouble.

I was at one of my lowest points when God brought Tracy into my life. She had a year of recovery under her belt, and I had maybe three hours, if that. The truth is, I was still smoking crack and using dope.

We were both at a recovery convention in South Florida. Tracy had driven two mutual friends, Chris and Carolyn, so that's how we were introduced. Everybody was hovering over me for pictures and autographs, but I was sick and frail. I'd lost so much weight my clothes hung off me like rags—she always says I looked like I weighed a hundred pounds soaking wet. My eyes were yellow, and I could barely sit up straight in my chair.

That whole scene disturbed her—the people there seeing me for what I'd been, not looking at me for what I was: a human being who needed help. This was 2003, and my baseball career was behind me. I was $3 million in debt and still without a driver's license after serving nearly a year in a Gainesville jail.

But we started talking, and we fell for each other. I told her not to get involved with me because I was still going through it myself—like my mother said I would—and I didn't want her to go through it with me. She stayed anyway, and I did take her through it.

That's about when Tracy called her parents in Missouri to tell them she was coming home . . . and bringing Darryl Strawberry with her. The same Mets player who once smashed a 440-foot homer off the clock at Busch Stadium, a shot that helped eliminate the Cardinals from playoff contention. She knew I couldn't stay in Florida with all its temptations and survive.

Tracy's mom and dad were great. But she was well ahead of me in her spiritual journey, and the Holy Spirit was telling her that continuing our relationship outside of marriage wasn't honoring God. She felt we couldn't keep living together under her parents' roof without getting married—and I wasn't ready.

We loved each other, but that wasn't enough. It was too unhealthy for Tracy. As someone in recovery, she couldn't put her life on hold while I sorted things out. It wasn't her job to rescue me.

She said, "You're going to have to grow up. You're going to have to be responsible and do it God's way."

For the sake of her restoration—and mine—she bought a plane ticket online and sent me to live with my godparents in California.

We hardly said a word on the way to the airport, and then we were apart for the first time in three years. Tracy on her journey with God in Missouri. Me, on my journey back in California.

I spent the next nine months studying the Bible, letting the Word pour into me.

I always say I got in line with God during that time, but it took work, and it took consistency. I remember God speaking to me, and He said, "The way you went after baseball, training and preparing for a season, you have to do the same thing when you spend time with the Word."

That was a turning point, when the two major parts of my life came together. I began to see it was all part of the same design. The discipline I'd built as a ballplayer laid the groundwork for me to learn the Word and become the man I was meant to be.

I firmly believe we all have a gift within us, but most people never use theirs. The way for me to get in line was to use my gift—the same one that took me out of South Central—and apply the discipline I'd used to become a great baseball player. God wasn't focused on my baseball career per se—not the stats, the home runs, or the stolen bases. But He used those playing days to shape me and lay the foundation for the man He wanted me to be.

What really mattered to Him was my soul and my salvation.

After almost a year apart, Tracy and I came back together and got married in a White Wedding Chapel in Las Vegas. No fuss, no frills. Just two people ready for a fresh start. She'd been renewing her life—reconnecting with friends in healthy relationships, attending church and Bible study, and going to recovery support groups. Meanwhile, she enrolled in college courses to pursue a career in real estate.

We started out with nothing and trusted God to rebuild us from the ground up.

And He did.

A week or so after the heart attack, I was at our lake house in Missouri, trying to regain my strength.

It's a simple, quiet spot, nothing fancy. When Tracy found the property, not far from our year-round home, it was in pretty rough shape and no one else saw its potential (kind of like me at the time we first met). But it's become an island of calm for us, and a getaway where we can be with family and friends or alone together. A place where all kinds of living things come to feel safe, with woods on three sides and deer roaming everywhere.

The deer aren't a bit scared of us. They'll mosey right up to the windows and watch us watching them, or roll around in the grass putting on a show. Tracy recognizes the different mothers and their fawns and scatters dried corn outside when the first snow falls and they all start looking a little thin. She has binoculars and bird books, and waits every year for the same pair of geese to come back, build their nest on the bank of the lake, and raise their goslings. She talks about the animals like they're members of our extended family.

"You see, she's looking for twigs."

"Where's her mate? Why are those two hawks circling every morning?"

"There's the doe with the bushy tail . . . She has two babies."

When I first came home from surgery, I was too weak to do anything but rest. The meds I was prescribed took me down a notch or two—lowered my blood pressure and slowed my heart rate so it wouldn't have to work too hard. But I felt drowsy and sluggish, like I was stuck in glue, and would end up sitting on the couch most of the day. I couldn't go out and preach. I was having trouble getting used to pacing myself. I had a defibrillator vest strapped around my chest to monitor my heart's rhythm and shock it back if it got too irregular. For the first time in my life, I truly understood why women hate wearing bras.

I wasn't the me I was used to being, and wondered if that had become my new normal. It was a depressing thought.

But after a few days, the old discipline took over. Tracy and I made a schedule: With spring here and the sky getting light earlier, I'd get up at 4 AM every morning and do Bible study. I spent hours with my Bible on my lap, reading pages with yellow highlights and worn edges from years of flipping back and forth. I focused on the passages about Jesus's powers of healing, like Matthew 9:2—"Then behold, they brought to Him a paralytic lying on a bed. When Jesus saw their faith, He said to the paralytic, 'Son, be of good cheer.'"

On April 30, I kept a fundraising date for Boys Town in Nebraska. It was a physical stretch for me, and I was still wearing the defibrillator. But too many adults had failed those young people and made them feel their lives weren't important. I needed to show up for the kids. Meet them, talk to them, and tell them they mattered.

Tracy doesn't usually travel with me, but under the circumstances, she came along and helped me get through it.

In early May, Tracy decided it was time for the next step in my medical recovery and bought me one of those golf putting mats—a strip of turf with a little cup at the end and a side chute that rolls the ball back to you.

I love golf, but didn't have the stamina or the doctor's okay to go out on the course. I needed to remember how to play and score once I got to the green. So, it was back to my familiar routine.

Discipline, preparation, reps.

Not long after that, I went to my doctor for a follow-up, took a stress test, and got great news: My heart function was normal and the defibrillator vest could come off. No more bra, yahoo! But the best part? I was cleared to go back to my Kingdom work—traveling around, sharing my faith, and loving on people.

The next day I stood by the lake and made a social media video to thank the thousands who'd sent me their prayers. It was one of those perfect spring mornings the Midwest blesses you with, blue blue sky, birds chattering, the water smooth as polished glass. I felt the sun on my skin like a kiss from above and clapped my hands, so much gratitude swelling inside me I could hardly contain it.

Next up? Citi Field in just over two weeks.

Glory to God for His grace and mercy!

And we're here. June 1, 2024, Citi Field. Fans in the seats, my teammates, wife, and children on the diamond.

I made it.

After everything, I'm here, listening as Howie Rose makes the introduction at Citi. I'm feeling honored, privileged, and most of all thankful the Lord has carried me to this special day.

"Back in 1980, the Mets had the first overall pick in baseball's annual draft. It was widely accepted that *Darryl Strawberry*, a high school senior from Los Angeles, was the best young player in the country . . ."

So many things race through my mind. I remember being in class when I found out I was drafted. My coach told me it was the New York Mets. I didn't know where New York was.

When the team was negotiating to sign me, they offered a $200,000 bonus so I'd give up my college scholarship. Then they flew me up East, and I saw the city for the first time. My mother came with me, and I was wearing a new suit that normally would have cost her half a month's pay. Ahead of the news conference, they played the Beatles song "Strawberry Fields Forever."

A few weeks later, I was in Tennessee with the team's Rookie-level affiliate, the Kingsport Mets. I couldn't have found that state on the map either. I'd never been in the Deep South—or even out of California—before all the fuss at Shea Stadium.

Best player in the country?

That wasn't how I felt back then. I knew the hype around my signing, and I felt like I was under a microscope. I was eighteen years old and billed as the Mets' savior. It was a lot of pressure.

I struggled mightily that summer, but the Lord put the right people in my life to help me through. There was my Rookie League manager, Chuck Hiller; my Class-A manager, Gene Dusan; and my A-ball teammate Lloyd "Big Mac" McClendon. Even then, I knew enough to recognize the positive figures around me, and to begin to see the value of true friendship.

I was drawn to the light, but blind to how to get there. I never dreamed *Jesus Christ* might have a plan and a purpose for me, if I could only let Him into my heart. It wasn't just about God showing up—it would take me surrendering, truly surrendering, to the Holy Spirit.

I would have to go through it. Mama knew.

"He was the National League's Rookie of the Year in 1983 . . . helped the Mets win the 1986 World Series . . . remains the franchise's home run leader, with 252 homers . . ."

As Howie rolls off those accomplishments from what could be

another life, it strikes me that the baseball diamond had been my sanctuary. The minute I put on the uniform, I could perform at the highest level. But once I stepped off the field, I was empty and broken.

How things have changed since then.

Just over a week ago at the lake house, a special gift arrived from the church we attend nearby, where Tracy's an active pastor and organizer. It's a beautiful photo collage—a single image made by combining two pictures: me in my Mets uniform dropping my bat on the left, and me preaching in a suit on the right. The camera's behind me in the preaching shot, and you can see I'm speaking to a large crowd.

In the middle of the collage there's a big circle with the number 18 inside, superimposed in Mets blue and orange. The circle's white, like a baseball, and inside are these words: *Acts 1:8—You will receive power when the Holy Spirit comes upon you, and you will be my witness to the ends of the earth.*

When I read that, it blew me away. The picture and verse together symbolize God's grace and purpose over my life—His redemption, and the mission that redemption confers on me. It told me the best part of my life is still to come.

I feel like I'm living it right now.

Out in the center field batter's eye, the Mets have turned the Home Run Apple—a BIG *Big Apple* that pops up whenever someone on the home team hits one out of the park—into a Home Run Strawberry for the day. I can't imagine how they did it, and don't even bother trying to figure it out. All I know is it's an awesome sight.

"Fans . . . please welcome the man we honor this afternoon . . . now and forever number 18, *Darryl Strawberry*!"

I guess my feet are on the ground as I approach the podium, but I can hardly feel them. It's like I'm floating out of the dugout. I hear the cheers and wish I could hug everyone in the ballpark, every person who prayed for me, forgave me, and loved me through all my mistakes, all the hurt I caused. But I can only open myself to the moment.

I move down the row where our blended family's sitting. Tracy's children, my children. Our children. We throw our arms around each other, and then I reach the end of the row and stop.

Tracy.

She looks me in the eyes, smiles, shrugs, and then kind of gestures me toward her. It's a look that shows me she's trying to hold back tears. A smile that says, *Well, what do you know—here we are.* She always had faith in us. God opened the door, but it still took a lot of dedication—and the two of us working through it together. And now that we're here, after all that hard work, for a heartbeat or two, it's just us, with God.

We embrace.

"We did it," I whisper against her cheek. "We did it, baby."

My wife and I stand in the bright sun, holding each other tight. Naturally, she's wiping the tears from my eyes. I have a speech to give.

Trace being Trace, she doesn't want my eyes too blurry to read my notes.

"Nothing like being home," I say into the microphone.

I hear my words over the PA. And I hear the crowd, almost forty thousand people, chanting: "Dar-ryl! Dar-ryl!" With the tears barely dry on my face, I smile ear-to-ear. If redemption's turning sorrow into joy, that's what this is all about. It's too easy to say it's a moment I'll never forget. It's a sacred moment, a testament to the love I found in Jesus Christ, a reminder of the grace that's chosen me, and of the weight of my transformation. I appreciate that transformation for everything it is—the full measure of what God has done in me, and the good that's come from it.

It really is about coming home.

I start by giving praise to God, thanking Him for His mercy, His love, and my life. Then I look down the line of honored guests. I thank the Cohens, the team's previous owners, the players—and I make it clear I'm celebrating *them* on this day that celebrates me.

Next, the fans.

"There was nothing like playing in Queens," I tell them. "Nothing like playing at Shea Stadium."

Their applause is the reason I'm about to get something off my chest . . . an apology I've owed them for the longest time.

My free agent year was 1990, and I'd gone into it after a down season in '89. The front office chose not to extend my contract and told my agent I would need to put up a good season before they made an offer.

I was angry, and their challenge hurt my pride. I'd given eight years of Major League service to the franchise. I was a kid from the ghetto, whose own father told me over and over that I was nothing.

I made up my mind that I would put up a good season, and I did.

I hit for a .277 average, with 37 homers and 108 runs batted in. I finished third in the National League MVP voting and made my seventh All-Star appearance.

At that stage of my life, I was unhealthy off the field, and I let my reaction come before any real reflection. I took that season with me and left to sign with the Dodgers, feeling my relationship with the team was broken . . . and it probably was, But I was broken, too, and that kept me from handling it in the best way possible.

Leaving was the biggest mistake of my career. I was accustomed to the intensity level of East Coast fans, and LA was more laid back. New York fans challenged me with their cheers and their boos. They made me better and pushed me toward my destiny. I would have never become the player I turned out to be without them pushing me.

And today, the number one thing I want to say to them is about that single biggest career regret.

I take a deep breath.

"I mean this from the bottom of my heart," I say. "I'm so sorry for ever leaving you. Truly, deeply sorry. I never played baseball for fans greater than you guys. And there was nothing greater than playing in front of you all those years."

The cheers are all I need to know they hear me—that they feel the truth of what I'm saying. The cheers tell me they're ready to move on, and it lifts a weight inside so I can move on too.

Being forgiven by thousands of people at once is an amazing thing.

I take a second deep breath, and thank my teammates—my band of brothers. Some of them are here on the field, and I name them all. But two I name together.

Mookie Wilson and Gary Carter.

They were always special to me—not just as guys playing baseball, but as examples of what a man should be, *what a man should look like.* They set the bar high.

One day during spring training, back in '89, I was walking around with a chip on my shoulder. I was angry and frustrated over the contract negotiations, feeling like I wasn't being respected. And Gary pulled me aside.

He said, "Straw, your life is about more than baseball. You think it's about a contract, you think it's about money, but it's not." Then he looked me straight in the eye and said, "God's going to use you mightily."

I remember thinking, *What is this dude even talking about?* My life *was* about the game and contracts. That's all I knew. But then he said something I never forgot. He said, "I don't tell a lot of folks this, but I'm telling YOU—you have a heart that's different."

That stuck with me. Even though I didn't get it at the time, something about what he said hit me deep inside.

I always say Gary and Mookie were drinking milk and I was drinking alcohol in those days—and it's true. While the rest of us were out partying after games, they were heading back to their hotel rooms, calling their families, and getting to bed early to be ready for the next day's game.

They led clean lives, and they lived under biblical principles. I saw that. And deep down inside, I wanted it.

Mookie once said that, as a man of faith in the game, you had to learn to live in two worlds. What he meant was that you had to be true to yourself and a man of character in both worlds. That planted something in me. A seed I didn't realize was there.

It took me a long road, full of mistakes, to finally understand how to live that way. But even when I was far from it, I could still see it was possible.

Mookie and Gary showed me that, and I believe I'm able to lead the life I have today partly because their example stuck with me.

The seed took its time, but it grew.

Gary's gone now, but his wife, Sandy, is here today. I turn to her, thank her for standing in his place, and thank her for what her husband meant to me—and to all of New York City.

Then I pause again as the wind flutters my notes. I flip to the page I want.

I look up toward heaven, my voice rising as the words pour out.

"Mom, I love you. Thank you for always praying for me. Thank you for always caring for me when I couldn't care for myself."

Later, I'll watch a video of the ceremony and hear the crowd rise alongside me. But in that moment, I'm caught up in speaking to her. I feel her looking down.

"You were always there in the middle, interceding for me. And I am always grateful, Mom. I will see you one day again."

I take a second to pull myself together and lower my eyes. I thank my in-laws and share the story of how my father-in-law, Jerry, dropped the phone when he heard a lousy, rotten Met was coming to live with them.

To my beautiful children, I repeat in public what I always tell them in private:

I love you.

To my wife—for the thousandth time—I say how grateful I am that the Lord gave me a spouse who pays more attention to me than I pay to myself. If it weren't for her, I might not be here today.

I'm almost finished. There's a Mets game to be played, and I'll be tossing out the ceremonial first pitch in my fancy suit, so I get to the heart of the testimony (feeling Tracy's heart as I say it): "The greatest gift I've ever received was accepting the Lord into my life—not just becoming a baseball player, but becoming a man."

It hits me that there's one last thing I need to mention. Because life is short, and you never know when it will be taken away.

"To you fans, and to the players of today," I say, "embrace this—it goes fast."

And with that, I'm done talking. For now.

I've still got that first pitch to throw . . . to my eldest son.

It's a strike. A 70 mph strike. But who's checking the radar gun for a cardiac patient?

After the ceremony, the Mets take care of me and my hungry bunch. There are plenty of us to feed. Besides my wife and kids on the field, I've invited nieces, nephews, grandkids, and friends, including pastors from across the country.

Tracy and I spend the next few days enjoying New York with the people we love, and it's a joy.

I'm blessed and energized. My physiology's adjusted to the new pace the heart medications set for it, and I hardly ever get that gluey sluggishness the meds caused early on. There are no more medical restrictions on my travel schedule moving forward. The doctors (and Tracy) just advise me to use common sense and pace myself.

My first ministry work after the number retirement is in a week. The day before, Tracy flies back to Missouri, and I'm off to Indiana to speak at an outdoor Christian music festival, where I tell a big crowd of young people about the part Jesus plays in my life. The next day, I'm up at a church near Albany, New York, giving testimony about my experiences, spreading some positivity on the weekend before Father's Day—and getting congratulated by a congregation full of Mets fans in number 18 jerseys.

Then I take a break and head home.

Trace and I treat ourselves to a date night in St. Charles and hang out at the lake house, napping under our snuggle blankets, lounging around barefoot on the couch, and watching the deer (we notice some have been giving piggyback—I mean, *deer*back—rides to little brown birds). While Trace is working on different projects at our church in Troy, I hang out with my golf club practicing my drives. I put a few balls in the lake, which tells me my strength is really coming back.

And, NO, I don't take any swings when Mr. and Mrs. Goose and their babies are paddling in the water.

Then I'm onto my first extended road swing since March.

The first stop is Seattle, Washington, where I speak at a fundraising banquet held by D.A.D.S.—the Divine Alternatives for Dads Services, a nonprofit organization with a mission that's especially dear to me, namely to end cycles of family violence and brokenness, and encourage fathers to become agents of change in their communities.

Next, I preach at a church in Pomona, California, on a very meaningful Father's Day. Just a few months before, I didn't know if I would ever see another, and still be around to take the calls and messages from the kids and grandkids. Then it's on to Baton Rouge, Louisiana.

My Kingdom work is back on with a AAA charge—like roadside assistance for the soul. I'm on call, running for Jesus with faith and passion.

It's what I love, what I was meant to do, and I'll keep at it for as long as He lets me.

Chapter Four

You Don't Need No Baggage

You know that spiritual "People Get Ready" written by Curtis Mayfield? It's about a train to Jordan coming to pick up passengers from coast to coast, and everyone's welcome to ride. You don't need a ticket, and you can leave your baggage behind. All you need to climb aboard is a little faith.

I think about that song as my travels lead me into Las Vegas, which isn't usually the first whistle stop on the ministry line. But I'll ride that train anyplace to share the Gospel and bring people where they need to be.

This is my first road trip of the New Year. After a break that stretched from Thanksgiving through the holidays, I'm bringing my mission a few miles from the Strip's neon lights, where I've been invited to speak at a conference for underrepresented entrepreneurs—Black, Latino, and other leaders—looking to balance their goals with fulfilling personal and spiritual lives. There's no actual ministering train to get me to the hotel, but I did pick up a Jeep Wagoneer SUV at the airport. Being a stretched-out, 6'6" former baseball player with a lot of wear and tear on my knees, I rent stretched-out vehicles with plenty of legroom to keep them from getting stiff.

My dear friend John Luppo's come along for the ride, and I want to tell you something about him.

Besides being a character, Johnny's faithful, trustworthy, and a fellow minister. He keeps me organized and manages my whole schedule on his calendar. When he isn't preaching, or praying his heart out for anyone he feels might be in need, he's acting on a TV series as a mobster's wheelman. If you can imagine Joe Pesci with a Bible, it's a pretty close fit. Every so often, he breakdances at fundraisers for causes he supports (he'll quote 2 Samuel 6:14, and remind you that King David danced before the Lord in prayer without holding back).

Johnny grew up in the Bronx and has the moves, the might, the Yankees cap, and the appetite for Arthur Avenue veal parm to prove it. He also has stories about growing up in a tough neighborhood and pulling himself out of trouble by the grace of God.

Back home in St. Louis, it's 30°, with a carpet of snow that's stuck around for weeks. Here it's a mild forty-eight degrees, pretty typical January weather for the Nevada desert. The air's crisp, and you see mountains wherever you turn.

Toward the end of November, Tracy had a major surgical procedure, and our daughter Alice came to spend time with us and help out with her recovery. That allowed me to make a brief trip to New York for an annual children's charity event that brought together people like my former Yankees manager Joe Torre, baseball Hall of Famer CC Sabathia, and others from different sports—including members of the Knicks and New York Liberty.

Then it was back home for Christmas. After a rough year, Tracy and I headed to Florida to visit our dear friends Pastors Ralph and Joanne

Hoehne, and Duane ("Dog the Bounty Hunter") and Francie Chapman. Tracy even managed to preach at Ralph and Joanne's Source Church. If you were in the congregation, the only sign she was still recovering from her operation was the few times she had to sit—though mostly, she was walking thunder. Just a few weeks earlier, she couldn't get around without a cane.

Tracy talked about what raised her spirits while she was laid up. "My doctorate can't help me on the couch," she said. When you're down, she told the congregation, it's not success or status that lifts you—it's faith. It's God working in you.

As I listened, her words reached deep inside me, and not because I'm her husband. I was a witness to her testimony, like everyone else there. She was still limping, still healing, but preaching like fire. She knew who she was in Christ.

I've heard her preach many times, but that day's words struck a different chord. I saw how fully God has anointed her and I was moved deep down inside. Her words weren't just inspiring; they were a testament to her purpose and the impact she has on everyone around her.

Tracy spoke about walking in holiness and obedience to God, how trusting His ways opens the door to His restoring power. When you live like that, you'll find hope, healing, and real purpose; Tracy has, because she's lived it. She's never just rolled over. Christ is her guiding light, and He never rolled over either. He is her strength, her example in adversity.

It's the kind of power that holds you up when nothing else can—not luxury cars, big houses, or designer clothes from Rodeo Drive.

That's the message I packed into my overstuffed suitcase and took with me to Las Vegas. You can be motivated, but it isn't enough. I didn't learn that when I played baseball—I learned it after my athletic career was over. I've had all the success and wealth anyone would want, but unless faith is present, everything else falls short.

But faith doesn't mean just letting things happen and leaving it to God. When the Holy Spirit is working inside you, there's an example to follow. God is always working—and we honor Him by working just as hard, letting His power move through everything we do.

Motivation plays its part—driving us to work toward our goals while staying true to God's principles. But it's living by these principles that encourages us to be different from those obsessed with having stuff.

I carry this message into the hall when I address those innovators and start-up leaders. I feel it connects with them, but my work doesn't end with my words to the large group. There's a roundtable discussion afterward in a small conference room off on its own. Quite a few people from the main assembly turn out. There's no moderator, microphones, no set topics. They can ask anything—business, personal, or even questions about my baseball life.

Some of it goes deeper than I expect.

Before I get to the roundtable, everyone has a chance to grab some lunch. Johnny and I pick the Raiders Tavern, a little sports detour where I can relax and get ready. The place is wall-to-wall silver and black, with helmets, jerseys, and multiple screens behind the bar playing Raiders, Raiders, and more Raiders—highlights, classic footage, and everything in between. There's even a corner with photos of Al Davis, watching over it all like a legend still calling the plays.

I grew up a fan, so this is the closest thing I get to a wild Sin City attraction.

As for what Raiders merch I pick up . . . well, that stays in Vegas.

At first, the roundtable discussion's familiar territory. People are always curious—they want to know about my baseball career and why I walked away instead of going into broadcasting or coaching like a lot of guys.

I don't mind. It's been over a quarter century since my last professional at bat, and I genuinely appreciate the interest. It tells me that, despite the old headlines about my struggles, people know I cared and never took the game for granted.

The second or third question takes us beyond baseball and straight to my purpose: *What made you decide to go from athlete to traveling evangelist, preaching the Gospel?*

I answer that I believe I was called a long time ago, and then talk about how my mother was praying behind the scenes—interceding for me, saying God would save me and knock me off my throne. After a while, it happened, and I answered the call.

I went through it, and He got it out of me.

But I want the young men in the room to understand that nothing was preordained. There are no guarantees. When you're lost in the darkness, any poor decision or misstep can change your destiny. I could have died of an overdose. I could have spent years in prison. My kids could have grown up without a father in their lives.

Things can fall apart so easily.

We're used to everything being wrapped up with a bow, like in a movie. The person finds himself in danger at the beginning, goes through all those twists and turns in the middle, and then comes out on top in the end. But in real life, it doesn't always work that way. You don't know how the story's going to turn out when you're in the middle of it. It's a hair's breadth between a happy ending and tragedy, and you're just trying to survive.

That was me. I didn't know how my story would end. I only knew how lost I was. When it came to finding God, it was like I'd put on a good pair of running shoes to take me in the opposite direction.

You can live like that for a while. There are all kinds of people around you whom you call friends, doing the same foolhardy, self-destructive things you're doing. But when you hit the storms of life, go through your troubles, they scatter like they were never there. And you realize they weren't really your friends. You start to understand the difference between the people who are along for the ride and the ones who actually care about you.

That's when I realized I needed to do something different. I didn't want to be in the tabloids anymore. I wanted to be a man like Moses and Peter in the Bible. They had issues, like the rest of us, but they found a way to walk with the Lord.

When you study the Bible, you learn God loves a man who walks in humility. That's the kind I wanted to be, and the road I wanted to walk. But finding that road was a very difficult challenge.

It was my wife, Tracy, who steered me toward it. I'd never met anyone who listened—really listened—the way she did. When I talked to her, she wasn't just waiting for her turn to say something. She was paying attention, hearing me, and trying to understand what she was hearing so she could help.

Everybody else was following me and slapping me on the back saying, "You're great, you're great." She said, "When are you going to take the uniform off and really find out who you are as a man?"

I was blown away. That was a heavy question. And it's when I started to figure out the answer that change came on.

In Vegas now, I look around the table in that little conference room. I see mostly men, thirties, competitive, successful. I know the type, because once that could have described me. A lot of young guys think they've got it figured out. They don't listen to advice, especially from women.

You can call it pridefulness, being an alpha, or whatever label people want to stick on it these days. I'm not saying every man does this, but let's be real: There are enough. Most guys deny it. But then they cut off a woman who's giving advice, or just tune her out like what she says doesn't matter, talking instead of listening.

God uses people to lead other people to their purpose, and He used Tracy to straighten me out. She's the biggest piece of my life, loving me right where I was when we met, and leading me back to the cross. Like a great coach or a manager, she's someone who has helped me perform and succeed at the next level. That's exactly what every coach did for me when I was playing baseball, and I'm grateful for it.

But the most important thing I learned from Tracy is to put yourself aside and really listen to what the other person's saying. For every healthy relationship, there's give and take, and it starts with listening. Ephesians 5:21 says, "Submit to one another out of reverence for Christ." To me, that's about deeply respecting the other person.

What I want to share with the young professionals around me is that becoming both a giving and receiving person changes how you approach every situation. The same qualities that make you a better partner in a loving relationship make you a stronger leader in business. In my case, they've made me a better minister.

The women at the table smile and look like they've been there. It's harder to read the men because we're conditioned to hold back our thoughts and feelings. One gives me a small nod, but the rest stay quiet.

"It's okay if the woman in your life straightens you out, guys," I say. A few have laughs that sound kind of nervous, and I see the hesitation in their eyes. I know Tracy saw the same hesitation in mine twenty years ago. "It'll make you a better man, not less of one."

There's a question about the work I do with the ministry. Somebody asks if I think things would have gone differently for my baseball career if I could go back in time, stick with Christ's principles, and live a cleaner life. I tell him the thing about life is that you can't go back.

"What's supposed to happen is supposed to happen," I say. "I think I would've made another fifty or sixty million dollars, won some more trophies, and never thought I needed God. If I hadn't fallen far enough, I never would've met Jesus."

The room gets a little still. There's a man to one side of me—well built, neat beard, sport jacket, white shirt with an open collar. He's been quiet and to himself since we started, like he's reflecting on something.

He clears his throat, his fingertips pressed together on the table.

"Forgiveness," he says.

The word's his way into something that we can all tell he has trouble bringing up. Everyone focuses on him and waits. "As a child, I was molested," he says, "I feel like it still haunts me every day."

This is the moment I told you about—the one where things go deep. Like I said before, it's unexpected in that setting. But I feel people reveal hard things to me because I talk about the hard things in my life.

At a lot of these events, the speakers—sometimes part of the hosting organization, sometimes Christian speakers—concentrate more on success, platforms, personal growth. There's a place for all that, and I'm not knocking them.

But I know as well as anyone that you can have all of it, be successful, well-known, respected—and still be broken.

I want to give this young man my best. To put myself aside and listen. I've just spoken to the group about Tracy doing that for me. Now I need to come through for him.

He says, "These gentlemen at this table, they've taught me that forgiveness is the biggest thing ever. But I still have a hard time." He grabs at the air with both hands, like he doesn't want the words to get away from him. "I need help . . . What can I do?"

I look him square in the eye. I can't heal him or take away what happened. But I can tell him the truth: that forgiveness is real, and I've wrestled with it too. That I kept my father out of my life for years because of what he did to me. And that my resentment and anger nearly killed me.

I don't go into the full story with the young man, and I won't here just yet. But I let him know that healing is possible. I tell him that God did it for me, and wants to set him free too.

But forgiveness is the key to it all.

He's sobbing as I speak. Some of the others at the table gather close, and lay hands on him, and he just cries harder. My heart goes out to him, but I know his vulnerability is a good thing—the first step toward opening up to God's healing. I tell him what was done to him isn't his fault.

That God loves him. That he doesn't have to carry that pain. And that he's going to be okay.

I say it because I've been there, and I want to give him comfort and encouragement. I say it because I'm another human being, and I know his struggle's real.

And I say it because I'm a minister, and this is truly what I live for.

I've got a few days after the conference until I need to hit the road—I'm making some appearances for the Mets in New York, then flying off to a California prayer summit for one of my favorite organizations, Victory Outreach, which gives hands-on help at rehabilitation among those affected by addiction and homelessness.

The summit isn't until early February; it takes a while for things to ramp up early in the year. But I don't mind the breather. I promised myself I'd take it slower after the heart attack, and I'm sticking to it.

I'm also getting back on the golf course—a real green with real grass and real pins. For the first time in months, I won't be just putting off a practice mat. The course is in Henderson, about sixteen miles from the resort. My godfather and a couple of friends are coming down from Los Angeles to meet me.

I know it's going to be a challenge. About ten months have gone by since the heart attack, and my strength is pretty much where it should be. But I still haven't gotten back my full stamina and endurance, and I'm just plain rusty using a club. I figure I'll have a hard time staying on the fairway.

All that said . . . I'm excited about stepping onto a course again.

I drive out the day after the conference and roundtable. Meanwhile, John Luppo's set to fly home to South Florida from Harry Reid International Airport.

We head north from the hotel—me in my SUV, Johnny in a car service. It's a half-hour trip for me on the highway, and I use it to reflect.

John, well, he has a moment worth sharing here, one I wouldn't hear about till later.

People open up to him all the time. On the way to the airport, he's talking to his driver, an older gentleman, who tells him about a family member who recently lost his life in a car accident. It's a horrible, tragic story, and as it pours out of the driver, Johnny can tell he's torn apart inside.

He prays for him in the car. He'll pray for anyone who might need it—friends, acquaintances, total strangers. Whoever he's praying for, he does it with all his heart. He asks for names and what the person would like him to pray for. He closes his eyes, bows his head, reaches out his hands, and gives it his all no matter where he is. In a hotel lobby, at a restaurant, on the beach, even at a Walmart Supercenter. Or the cart corral outside.

Before John leaves the car, the driver says he felt the Holy Spirit there in the drop-off lane in front of the terminal.

Don't look for me to be surprised. I don't love the guy for nothing.

Chapter Five

Be Still, and Know That I Am Golf

Did I mention golf?

Chimera Golf Club is a beautiful regulation course tucked into the desert foothills, with lakes, ponds, palm trees, acres of Bermuda grass—and that big dragon statue near 9, kind of like my appetite after a round.

Par's 70 to 72—not that I worry about it. I'm rusty anyway. I'm also very competitive, but I've tamed the savage athlete in me. I don't go out there trying to be Tiger or Jack Nicklaus. My attitude is that playing golf makes me a better preacher. *How?* I'll explain in a minute. The way I see it, though, that's the real win.

I picked my playing partners—my godfather and a close friend of many years—so it would stay relaxed. No pressure. Just go out, play a little, and have some fun.

On the interstate up through Henderson, I think about the roundtable and that young man who told me what he'd been through. Once people realize I'm not going to judge them, they start sharing things they've never said out loud.

I don't take that as a burden. Ministering is serious business—it carries a huge responsibility. Not to man, but to God Himself. God's using me as His vessel, and I'm thankful for the privilege. I want to represent Him the right way.

But there's real pain that comes pouring out of people. That guy was truly struggling.

I'm still human. It stays with me. And that brings me to the biggest reason I love golf: It pulls me away for four or five hours. No phone, no email, no internet. Just space to breathe. It helps me relax and reset.

And it isn't just the quiet. Golf's a real challenge, and we all need that in our lives. I'm not saying a good round fixes everything—but it conditions you. Sharpens the tools you need to handle life better.

For me, it's most enjoyable to be out on the course with good friends. It's more peaceful, and helps me keep my competitive side in check.

I never let it eat at me when I don't play well. Instead, I try to take in the nature around me. You might run into deer in some places, alligators if you're in Florida (don't worry about me turning into a 6'6" gator biscuit—they want to crawl off and hide if you give them the chance). Anyway, on the course you can break away from every aspect of life and not think about a thing.

I played baseball for seventeen seasons. I trained year after year, going to the gym, lifting weights to maintain my body. It's no longer important to me to have the physique I did back then. I really just want to stay active and healthy.

I've got bad knees from sprinting, stopping, diving, and sliding. Shoulder problems from crashing into walls. But I still get out there and push myself. Golfing is good all-around exercise—cardiovascular, strength, balance, and flexibility—and I'd rather play a good, tough round than ever set foot in a gym again.

I knew a few guys from my Major League days who used to play golf. Looking back, I'd say the majority were starting pitchers since they only pitched about once a week. Everyday position players—who were out on the field a hundred, a hundred-fifty games a season—would've been too worn down from playing. Most nights, I wouldn't even wander into my hotel room until 3 AM, when the partying was finally over. Get up at six to play golf and start lugging my clubs? If you were living like I did on the road, there was NO way.

I took up golf after my ballplaying days were over, bringing with me all the aches, pains, and worn-out joints that came with the game. I never walked onto the course thinking I was on the PGA Tour or about to launch a three-hundred-yard drive like the pros. My body knew better, even if my ego still wanted to be the boss. And I'm not saying Mr. Ego Strawberry wasn't whispering in my ear, telling me I could do it.

That's a big word, ego, though it's only three letters. I like to say they stand for Easing God Out. You ease God right out, and you play at being God yourself.

I don't recommend it.

When I think about what I could do when I was younger—not just on the baseball field, but on the basketball court and high school football gridiron—I could be tempted to swing for a hole-in-one, even though I've got no business trying. I'll never forget what I could do with a thirty-three-ounce bat, never forget how it felt vibrating in my hands after I sent a ball sailing over the fence. Every man who's ever stepped onto a golf course has I-can-win-the-Masters daydreams. When you're a former power hitter, those daydreams can be epic.

But like the Bible says, pride comes before the fall. Just ask David where all Goliath's bragging and hotdogging got him, friends.

Now let's go deeper.

For me, golf is about control. Mental, emotional, physical, and spiritual control of *myself*, not anyone else. When one of those four is off, the other parts feel it. And when they line up? That's when things really come together. When *that* happens, it's like gas in the tank. It keeps you moving forward and growing in step with God.

I already mentioned that golf's a challenge. The fairway might be big, but keeping the ball on it is trickier than it looks. There are hills, wind, bunkers, water—and the pressure you put on yourself not to mess up. Even guys who've hit World Series home runs have to work to keep the ball out of the woods.

That's where Staying and Playing comes in. I already mentioned my bad knees, and how my shoulder acts up sometimes from old injuries. But we all have aches, pains, bumps, and bruises—and we all owe it to ourselves to push through. In baseball, you've got to handle ballparks of different shapes and sizes, account for the weather, and figure out whether the home plate ump has a tight or wide strike zone. In golf, it's the same type of challenge. You're battling yourself, the course, and the people you want to beat. Testing your body's endurance, toughness, and ability to perform.

You're also testing your mental strength. If you don't play consistently, it's going to be tough every time you go out. If your mind's not strong and focused, you lose sight of the fact that you're there to have fun, and that can make for a long, long day.

I never want to feel down after playing golf, even if I stink it up. Feeling bad defeats my purpose, and that's why I try not to let frustration get the best of me.

I don't curse, even when I hit a bad shot. I never let the f-bombs fly. This isn't to judge any of my potty-mouthed golf buddies. I've been around athletes my whole life. I came up in Crenshaw—cussing ain't new to me! But I'm a preacher now, and have been for almost twenty years. That means everything. I've got to hold up my end of the bargain with God and carry myself right.

Is it tempting to toss a club at a tree sometimes? Sure. But I don't want to scare an innocent little bird. I don't want to look back and remember that was how I conducted myself.

As a preacher, I'm accountable on or off the course. Walking with God isn't something you only do when it's convenient. You have to be consistent. For me, that walk has to stay steady whether I'm home, preaching, or knee deep in the rough.

And that connects to the spiritual part. You can always find a reason to turn this way or that off the path. Every step is a choice. If I keep my mind strong, and don't give in when negative thoughts and feelings pull at me, I'll stay spiritually strong. When I miss a shot or things go sideways on the course, I still have to be an example. That's part of the calling, and it's part of growing.

It's not losing sight of who I am.

As for my round at the Chimera: I hate to disappoint anyone, but there's no great story. I've been out on a golf course somewhere in America at least a dozen times since then, and I don't have great stories about those outings either.

That's really why I'm writing about it here. The golf course is a *break* in the story. It's pushing "pause." There's no drama.

It can be this way for all of us, if we choose not to take things too seriously. We just have to keep our perspective.

Golf—or any outdoor activity—is a great way to get outside and clear your head. We all need fresh air and sunshine once in a while, whether it's for a walk, a swim, a run, or a few holes.

Life isn't easy. Everybody has pressures wearing at them. Being out in the sun for half an hour boosts your vitamin D, which helps your body fight off infection. It also triggers your brain to release serotonin—a hormone that lifts your mood and helps you feel more balanced.

What this means is the benefits from outdoor exercise are a bonus. God created our beautiful world so we get healthier just soaking it all in.

And often, the things we enjoy that are good for us can do more good than we realize.

I fit as many charity outings as I can into my schedule. Over the past few months, I've done charitable golf events that brought me together with dear friends from baseball, ministry, and everyday life. I played in outings for Tunnel to Towers, helping 9/11 first responders dealing with health problems from that terrible day; for an organization supporting autistic children on Long Island; at a Florida tourny raising awareness for young women facing addiction and trafficking; for another benefiting pediatric and adolescent psychiatry programs.

With so many good causes, I keep trying to squeeze in more.

I guess you could say golf isn't just a break from life for me. It's part of life. It makes me more patient, checks that EGO whenever it rears up, and gives me time to think and reflect. It even helped get me off the couch after the heart attack.

Whether I'm out with friends getting behind a cause or trying not to whack myself in the foot with an iron, I make sure to stay true to myself, walk with faith and purpose, and keep my heart open to what God's still teaching me, learning from my mistakes on and off the fairway.

The book of Ecclesiastes tells us, "*The end of a matter is better than its beginning, and patience is better than pride.*"

I can't say it any better. In fact, with a line that perfect, I won't try.

Like any sensible golfer who's had a fine day on the course, I know when to put away the clubs and look forward to the next round.

Chapter Six

Another Life

"It's a celebration of you having another life.
Of all of us being here together."
—Mead Chasky, sports memorabilia agent and collector

It's March 8, four days and counting to my birthday, and I'm heading from frozen St. Louis to Florida's Atlantic coast, where the Mets are deep into spring training at Clover Park in Port St. Lucie.

This is my second year in a row as a guest coach. Even before the organization retired my number, Steve Cohen reached out to invite me to preseason camp and other team events. But with the COVID pandemic's contact restrictions and my schedule as a minister, 2024 would be my first year at camp under his ownership.

I'm glad to be back.

Spring training's special to me. It's a chance to connect with young players, and reconnect with Mets longtimers—teammates, announcers, clubhouse guys, security people, the list goes on. It's also a chance to show my appreciation to fans face-to-face: the older ones who remember my playing days, and the young kids and teens who hear about those memories from their parents

It amazes me how people remember the crack of my bat when I hit a particular home run, how the ball traveled in the air, where it landed in the stands. They'll go on about the opposing team, the score, who was on base, and exactly where they were sitting: left, right, or center; field level or nosebleeds. They love the game, and travel thousands of miles so they can escape the tail end of winter and see past and present players close-up.

I always like sharing a few words with someone, or stopping for a snapshot and a handshake. I want fans to know how much their love and support over the years still means to me, and I want to give some of that love back. Baseball ties people together at a time when they seem ready to fight it out over everything—culture, medicine, politics, you name it, we can yell at each other over it. But the ball that hit the clock at Busch Stadium with the '85 pennant on the line? Whether you're a die-hard fan or were on the team that year, thinking about it makes you smile. Doesn't matter how you feel about those other things.

As a traveling evangelist and former baseball player, I've come to see that those two sides of my life are more harmonious than you might think. The Reverend Billy Graham, whom I always respected, was close to presidents from both political parties, and had lifelong friendships with all different types of people. Somebody once said of him: "He was preaching from the books of the Bible, which are hundreds, if not thousands, of years old, and yet the message is relevant because the human heart remains the same."

Those words really speak to me.

There was a time when my healing process meant distancing myself from my baseball legacy (*Take off the uniform*, remember?). Before I could reclaim it, I had to be sure my priorities were in balance. I aimed to be standing on good, solid, level ground.

That's to say, spiritual ground. These days, I'm steady on my feet. I know who I am, and I know the purpose God's laid out for me. It's made all the different parts of my life come together.

Baseball's a piece of the puzzle, maybe a whole section. When I realized where it fit into the big picture, when I really understood, I could put the game in its rightful place.

I'm still in this world to be an instrument of my Christian faith. A good husband, father, grandfather, and friend. That's it. The entire reason I was saved. But being able to once again reclaim and embrace my legacy as an athlete is something for which I'm profoundly grateful. It gives me a platform for reaching people with my message of hope and restoration.

With my heart attack in the early spring, and then Tracy's surgery, this year's invite to camp is extra welcome. It comes not long after my baseeball family lost one of its all-time greats.

Right before our Christmas with friends—when Tracy preached at their church—I heard about the passing of baseball Hall of Famer Rickey Henderson. As the calendar turned toward spring training, I couldn't help thinking about him.

Rickey was one of the best offensive players of his era—a sly base stealer, great hitter, and, above all, a total, hard-nosed gamer. He crackled with electricity, like a ten-million-volt battery. Rickey and I were both outfielders back when I was with the Dodgers and he was on the Oakland Athletics. We once had fun posing together for a baseball card that showed guys who played the same position (they called it an Oddball card—and I'll leave it to you to figure out why!). Over the years, our paths often crossed at signings, and we always had a lot of laughs.

It was a real shock when Rickey passed. Back in the day, we called him the Man of Steel because of his ability to stay on the field even with nagging injuries. He'd looked in great shape back in September, throwing out the first pitch when the A's played their final home game in California before moving to Las Vegas.

Losing him was a reminder that none of us are guaranteed another day, and that we need to cherish each one and make it count for something.

God gives us time, and we honor Him by how we spend it.

Okay. March 2025. Spring training.

I land in Port St. Lucie on a Saturday evening and get a good night's sleep at my hotel. Sunday, I wake up raring to go and drive the five miles to the ballpark in my latest rental, a fully loaded Suburban big enough for a family of manatee. The closer I get to Clover Park, the more I feel the excitement stirring inside me. It's the golden sunshine pouring through the windshield, the palm-lined entry lane to the parking area, the Mets staffers I've known for decades—people who've shared their lives' biggest milestones with me—showing off their latest grandkid snaps as I pull up to the gate.

Outside, the air has a fresh, crisp bite, and those seabirds you never see anywhere but Florida (but that Trace could probably name) are gliding overhead in the breeze. I soak it all up as I leave the clubhouse in my spring training uniform—a blue top with long orange sleeves, white pants with blue and orange piping.

For the next hour or two, I watch batting practice, assist with outfield drills, talk to a few up-and-coming prospects who've been invited to try out for the Major League club, and do some media interviews. The team has a top-notch coaching and training staff, and players like sticking to their set workout routines, so I try not to get in the middle, where toes can be stepped on. The best thing I can do is share my experience, and encourage them to relax, enjoy the company of their teammates, and have fun.

Not too sabermetric right there. I get it. But it's what I know. And it's how you form the camaraderie that holds a team together through the good times and rough stretches of a long baseball season.

That evening's game runs almost three hours, and when it's over, I'm ready to grab something to eat and turn in. I loved every minute of my first day at the park, but it was a long one.

Monday night I'm back for a sellout against the St. Louis Cardinals. I talked earlier about how the Cards were our hated archrivals in my time, and there's still some juice left in the matchup. With less than three weeks until Opening Day, team rosters are taking shape and the games have more of a regular-season feel.

This game airs live in New York, and between the 2nd and 3rd innings, I'm mic'd up to talk to the Mets broadcasters—my buddies and former teammates Keith Hernandez and Ron Darling—along with field reporter Steve Gelbs, who's sitting in for play-by-play announcer Gary Cohen (no relation to the team's owner).

Keithy sounds primed to break my chops, and I play along. He was like an older brother when we were teammates, and that hasn't changed. "*Straaaaw-man!* You're a birthday boy soon, huh?"

I let him know he's right. Wednesday's March 12. We're at birthday minus two. I'm about to turn sixty-three.

"I remember when you were *twenty*!" he says.

"Imagine." I laugh.

We go back and forth, talking baseball. Steve Gelbs asks how I feel about Pete Alonso, the recently re-signed first baseman, getting close to breaking my team home run record. I tell Steve I'm rooting for him. Records are meant to be broken.

"I've been holding it for thirty-seven years," I say. "He's a homegrown player . . . Go get it, Pete!"

Ron closes out the segment by bringing up the Mets' old feud with the visiting Cards, and I remind him things were more heated back in the day, because of the trade for Keith. We reminisce a little more, and then, in a flash, my spot's over.

It was a fun few minutes—and leave it to Keith to remember my birthday. But he isn't alone. My friend Mead Chasky (I'll get right back to him) has been hinting he has something in the works. Also, Jay Horwitz is in town and he's invited me for dinner tomorrow night.

Then it hits. Tracy always says it isn't important to be important, and that's become one of my mottoes. What's important is to recognize the moments that teach us life lessons, and take what we can from them.

I turn back to the baseball diamond, lean out over the dugout rail, and watch the action on the field. I'm thinking that *tomorrow*—March 11, the day before my birthday—is as big and important a date as they come, given what happened on this day last year.

The next morning, I wake up early again to head over to Clover Park. But this time I have company waiting down in the hotel lobby.

Mead Chasky's the guru of sports and entertainment memorabilia—and a dear friend. There are autograph agents, and then there's Mead. He isn't just a promoter; he's an original who started out as a trading card collector, turned the thing he loved most into a living for himself, and became one of the guys who created the multibillion-dollar industry from the ground up.

Mead and I have known each other over four decades, since before the '86 Mets team won the World Series. Over the years, I've come to realize his crusty exterior hides a lot of depth. Like with most longtime relationships, ours has seen some ups and downs, but we've learned from our experiences and gained a lot of trust through it all. I think our bond's gotten stronger because of it.

Or *maaaybe* I'm just stuck with him, like with family.

Anyway . . .

Half the team's off on a split-squad road game, and there's no game scheduled at Clover today, leaving the rest of the players to take drills and BP. That equals a short day at the ballpark, so Mead's arranged for me to do a signing after I'm finished there.

"I'm tired," he says with a yawn as we head out to the SUV.

"It's eight o'clock in the morning," I say. "How can you be tired?"

I don't really expect an answer. Mead hustles from the minute he wakes up—and also enjoys the nightlife, to put it mildly. I'm usually in bed by 8:30 PM. In that way, we're total opposites. But once upon a time we would've been hanging out at all hours. He remembers the person I used to be, and respects who I've made myself into with the help of God and my wife. When he sees Trace, he always calls her a miracle worker. That mutual respect's a big reason we get along so well. I don't try to change or impose my faith on my friends, or even my kids. I just live it out and hope I can be an example by walking the walk.

I believe lasting relationships are about giving people our respect and attention. Life gets busy for all of us, but I consciously make time for my loved ones, because God made time for me. I find that if we pay attention to them, they'll talk to us about the things they need to talk about. Either that or they'll circle back when they're ready.

As I drive us to breakfast, Mead's on the phone making and answering calls and leaving messages. He's on the phone between forkfuls of scrambled eggs at the restaurant, and stays on all the way to the ballpark.

"Shef, you going to be in Tampa for the show?"

"Tony O., what's up?"

"Lou, I heard your song on the radio—it reminded me of something. Get back to me . . ."

That's Gary Sheffield, the ballplayer, and the singer Tony Orlando, and Lou Gramm, cofounder and original front man of the rock band Foreigner. Mead knows and represents people from every walk of life. The ones who answer him now at eight thirty in the morning all sound cranky, and I'm ready to bet they're giving their phones the stink-eye.

"Maybe you should call them a little later," I say.

Mead shrugs. "Hey," he says, and taps in another number. "I'm making things happen!"

I swing off I-95, and we're at the park before nine. The clubhouse is restricted to players and coaches, and there's about an hour to kill before the field opens to visitors. Mead tells me he'll wait in the SUV till it warms up outside.

"Man, it's cold this morning," he says. He tugs at his short sleeve—in case I haven't noticed it's short. "Think you can borrow a hoodie from the clubhouse?"

He reaches into his shirt pocket for a big, fat stogie. As anyone who meets him finds out, Mead loves his cigars. In fact, he's a legitimate connoisseur. He even owns a cigar lounge around the corner from Yankee Stadium.

"I don't want you stinking up the SUV," I say, and nod at the Junko in his hand.

"What's wrong with cigars?" He sounds like Queens, New York, where he grew up.

"They smell nasty," I say. "And they're bad for you."

He looks down at the huge cigar, then looks up at me and shakes his head. "You used to smoke cigarettes."

Imagine you're stuck in a TV comedy rerun you've watched a hundred times. One where you know every line by heart.

"Used to," I say. "I quit years ago."

"Cold turkey, right? But cigarettes are worse for your health. When you smoke them, you inhale. A cigar, you don't."

Did I say Mead's like family to me? Maybe I should've compared him to bubbles in still water. Picture yourself looking out at a peaceful, quiet pond—like at my lake house. All of a sudden, the surface starts bubbling and churning. Doesn't matter why. The water's stirred up, and the geese get bothered and leave. Goodbye peace and quiet.

"If you light that thing, do it outside," I say, and leave him to wait in the passenger seat.

Even with half the team gone, it's a busy day on the field. Mead eventually shows up and hangs out in the dugout, while I watch Francisco Lindor, Pete Alonso, and Juan Soto take their swings under the batting net and imagine what a triple threat they'll be in the lineup. Soto just signed a historic fifteen-year contract, and he's worth every cent; no one else in the game has his approach to hitting. I've already mentioned my hopes for Alonso, and Lindor's a spark plug and natural leader—the kind of unselfish player a team gels around.

I share some private words of appreciation with Lindor before he heads from the dugout into the clubhouse, one generation paying it down to the next.

"Think I could get a picture with him, Darryl?" Mead asks behind me.

The signing's at 1 PM, and we head over after stopping for lunch at my favorite local soul food place. Fried catfish, greens, seasoned yams and cornbread, mmm-mmm.

"We're looking for a convention hall," Mead says as we pull onto the road. "Something like that."

His navigation app takes us to a typical Florida-style shopping center, with tan facades and a massive parking lot. I slow-cruise past a karate school and deli. No convention hall.

"You sure this is the right place?" I ask.

Mead shakes his phone in my face. "That's what it says!"

But he doesn't sound too confident and turns to look back out the window. Then he jabs his finger at a plain glass storefront a couple of doors down from the deli, and next to a preschool. The painted lettering on the door says: *Event Center. All your event needs. Bar and bat mitzvahs, corporate meetings, life celebrations, graduations . . .*

Nothing about baseball events. But then one of the organizers steps out, spots us, and waves us toward a parking spot.

"Darryl, Mead, welcome!" He holds open the door.

Inside, we see long rows of tables loaded with game-used jerseys, caps, leather gloves and mitts, sneakers, balls, bats, batting helmets, and baseball cards. Hundreds and hundreds of cards to be autographed by me and other players from Mets camp. All exactly what you'd expect at a sports signing. But there are also fancy chandeliers hanging over the aisles and artificial trees in back. The trees reach almost to the ceiling, their branches bushy with white blossoms.

Mead points. "What's with them?"

The organizer tells him they're Japanese cherry blossom trees.

"And those things?" Now he's looking up at the crystal light fixtures.

"Chandeliers."

Mead makes a face. "I mean, what are they doing here? Somebody getting married?"

"Actually, the wedding was yesterday," the organizer says. "A rabbi married the couple under those trees. They're supposed to bring good luck—it's very sweet."

Mead's face screws up tighter and the organizer shrugs. "We're lucky to have this place! Spring training, everything in town's booked up."

While they talk, one of the staffers slides a chair over to me, passes me a Sharpie, and hefts my first box of cards onto the table. There are some 350 cards to a box. I have a lot of signing to do before we even get around to the baseballs.

Soon the players come trickling in from the park. Soto, Alonso, Jeff McNeil, and some other guys. They all get handed Sharpies and heaps of collectibles to sign. There's a whole system in place to keep things running smoothly, and two MLB authenticators verifying each item with an official silver holotag.

The authenticators are serious about what they do and impress me with the pride they take doing it. These are the same people that collect home run balls, bases, lineup cards, mound dirt—you name it—to validate on the spot at the ballpark. Most are off-duty law enforcement types, used to following chain-of-custody evidence procedures. The game is all about 150 years of history, and they're the men and women keeping it real.

It's about three in the afternoon when we leave the Event Center. The memorabilia people have been great but my fingers hurt. I could use a break and a shower before Jay's get-together.

Mead whips out a cigar when I drop him off at his hotel. I have to smile and shake my head. I can't make him quit, but that doesn't mean I won't stay on him about it.

Something tells me Billy Graham would understand.

Jay's dinner is a bigger affair than he let on. I should have expected it. He'd told me he was flying back to New York tomorrow and didn't want to miss my birthday.

I've known everyone at the table forever. There's our close friend Linda; the Mets' head of PR; their visiting clubhouse manager; the minor league affiliate's play-by-play announcer; and the guy who runs the team's video operations. Rounding out the party are Mead and his phone.

It's an Italian feast. We talk, laugh a bunch, and catch up on one another's lives as we pass around serving trays piled with mountains of appetizers. Prosciutto, scungilli, shrimp, lobster tails, and bruschetta.

After the main course, our servers set a huge platter of cannoli down in front of me. There's a candle sticking up from one of the pastries, and I know what's in store. Before I can make a wish, the staff's behind me singing "Happy Birthday." One of them booms it out in a big Pavarotti voice.

As I close my eyes and puff my cheeks, I silently thank God for another year of serving His will and walking the path that's been laid out for me. Another year of life, and making the best of what's left, however long I'm given.

Then I blow out the candle. Everybody claps and holds up their glasses (water for me). I'm smiling as we toast, but it's a serious kind of smile, and someone notices.

"Today's a year since we almost lost you, right?"

I nod. It is. A year since Tracy sped me to the hospital with what felt like an iron clamp squeezing my chest. Since I almost died of a major coronary.

Exactly one year.

That thought's been knocking at the back of my mind lately, and now it's stepped right in—like an uninvited guest at the table.

"What do you call a day like this?" the person asks. I won't embarrass him by saying who. "Anniversary doesn't feel right somehow."

I get his meaning. To me, that word fits the festive occasions listed on the Event Center's door—weddings, bar mitzvahs, brisses, graduations. Under the artificial cherry blossom trees.

I sit there, trying to come up with a better word.

Someone else chimes in, "How about we just say today marks the date?"

That doesn't cut it either. It sounds flat, like it's in a history book. I want a word that expresses what the occasion really signifies to me.

I'm still thinking it over when Mead, who's been listening to all this, leans in from my side.

"It's a celebration of you having another life," he says. "Of all of us being here together."

I sit there looking at him. *Celebration of another life.* He hit it. The sweet spot. The perfect words—and then some.

Mead grabs a cannoli and downs half of it in one bite. He's got a big grin on his face. Suddenly, I do too.

I told you he's not just the guy with the phone.

Chapter Seven

Don't Point . . . Pray

Angola Prison, Louisiana

"Freedom is not a destination. It's a journey. It's a daily choice."
—Tracy Strawberry

On a warm Southern morning two weeks after spring training wraps, I'm on Interstate 61 north of Baton Rouge, Tracy beside me in the passenger seat of a Jeep Grand Wagoneer with a smooth ride and a cruise ship's worth of space. After a hotel breakfast, we've set out for the Louisiana State Penitentiary in a secluded part of West Feliciana Parish.

Baseball was a good break, but now I'm back to the serious work of ministering.

Called Angola by locals and inmates, the maximum-security prison stands on land that was part of the Angola cotton plantation before the

Civil War. They say the plantation was named after the African nation where the slaves forced to labor in the fields came from.

We've partnered with a Christian outreach group, God Behind Bars, for our visit. With a strong record working with penal institutions, the group arranged a full day's program at the facility. Its young volunteers come from all across the country, and we're grateful for everything they've done in advance. But heavy thunderstorms have set them behind schedule. There were long layovers, late arrivals, and even some kind of snag involving a guitar one of them is bringing along.

With so many flight delays, Tracy and I decided to get rolling ahead of the rest. The drive to the prison compound's about sixty miles, and at first the roadside is what you'd expect on any highway in America—gas stations, fast-food restaurants, shopping centers, quiet planned suburbs with modern homes and neat green lawns. It isn't until we pass the Exxon oil refinery, with its giant tanks and high stacks puffing white smoke into the sky, that it feels like the Deep South.

When the scenery changes, it changes fast, and we're in the Louisiana countryside: seventy-foot-tall cypress trees, climbing vines, bungalows with porches and columns, and mobile homes, some with rusty cars perched on cinder blocks in their yards. Our GPS tells us to take a left onto LA-66, a two-lane blacktop that stretches across an old steel truss bridge into miles of hills, cow pastures, and woods so thick it's hard to see any sunlight peeking through the brush.

The God Behind Bars team texts that they're on the way, but there's no one in my rearview mirror, and only a few pickups come rumbling toward us.

I drive on through miles of twists, turns, and scattered farms on either side. We pass a tiny white-steeple church, then a general store a few hundred yards up ahead.

I nod toward the store. "Great location."

Tracy turns to look. "Why's that? There's hardly anything else around here."

"There's the church," I say. "People can grab lunch for the cooler after the service."

She smiles. "Leave it to you."

I rub my stomach. Though I can't vouch for other ministers, I burn off a lot of calories when I preach, and always feel starved afterward.

The road runs through more backwoods. Every so often we see a farmhouse standing in a field. But then it disappears behind us, and we're hemmed in by trees again.

It's no accident the prison's in such an isolated location. An inmate who manages to escape would have to hike through miles of forest and bayou, or swim across the Mississippi River, before finding a roof to shelter under. That's with K-9 handlers tracking him on the ground, helicopters and heat-seeking drones searching from the air, and wild pigs, gators, and rattlesnakes roaming the forest at night in the pitch darkness.

And about those guard dogs—years ago, Angola crossed black wolves and German shepherds for its corrections officers, and its kennels still hold some of the hybrids.

There's nowhere to run or hide out here.

As we get close, I look over at Tracy in the passenger seat. She's quiet and still, and I don't just mean on the outside. In our moments of stillness, God's voice often speaks to us the loudest, and I can see the purpose and reverence in her eyes. Tracy's getting ready for what we've come to do, trusting the Holy Spirit to center and guide her in reaching out to the souls behind the prison's entrance.

There's a redbrick sign above a bed of pretty flowers in front of the lowered vehicle barrier. We might mistake it for a recreational campground if not for the words: **LOUISIANA STATE PENITENTIARY**.

The roof above the checkpoint also announces the name of the prison, and past it we see a sniper tower and tall chain-link fences topped with razor wire. One way in, one way out. And for inmates, there's usually no way out.

As we pull up to the guardhouse, I pass our driver's licenses out my window to a Correctional Assistant Warden-4 named Riley. She's friendly, prepared, and has kept in touch with the God Behind Bars team—whom she tells us are still about ten minutes back on the road.

AW-4s at Angola are senior officers. Riley and another female correctional officer, Master Sergeant Ellie Brooks, will be our escorts.

Tracy and I are prescreened and don't need to be patted down. But the prison guards inspect all arriving vehicles for contraband—no exceptions. As we step outside to wait, my eyes drift past the checkpoint to some parked cars, a full-size prison bus, and a couple of monster 4x4s that make the Wagoneer look like a compact hatchback. They're white with black *Louisiana Corrections* insignia on the doors and steel mesh panels over the side and rear windows.

The sniper tower and fencing past the vehicle pool tell us we're about to leave the world of the free. That world dead-ends at the stop sign and lowered gate where LA-66 runs up to the prison entrance. The other side's a world of enforced confinement and discipline, of pain and sorrow—and for some, remorse and repentance. If you live there and don't belong to the correctional staff, it's because you've been locked up for committing a serious crime. In most cases here, that's murder, rape, or armed robbery.

When Riley finishes her search, we get back in the Wagoneer and the barrier rises to let us through. Officer Brooks—she asks us to call her "Ellie"— pulls one of the prison's 4x4s alongside us, lowers her window, and smiles. We see that same warm, lively smile throughout the morning and afternoon. Louisiana born and bred, she's nothing like the movie stereotype of a hardcase prison guard.

"Y'all follow me," she says. "I'll lead you to the main building while the rest of the group catches up."

I notice Tracy taking a phone video as Ellie leads us in over a dirt road.

"Unbelievable, right?" I ask.

She nods. "Twenty-eight miles . . . It's hard to wrap my head around."

I remember feeling the same way my first time here, about a year ago. What sets Angola apart from other prisons starts with its size.

Angola covers 28 square miles and 18,000 acres. For perspective, compare that to the city where I played baseball for 13 years. Manhattan Island spans 22 square miles and 14,000 acres, making Angola larger by 6 square miles and 4,000 acres. If you dropped Manhattan over the prison like the lid of a fry pan, you'd still have room around it for two Central Parks—besides the one under the pan lid. And Central Park, with its lakes, waterfalls, fields, woods, and zoo, is so big and sprawling that most lifelong New Yorkers have never explored all of it.

Next, Angola's considered a prison farm—the largest operation of its kind in America. Cotton, corn, sugarcane, soybeans, mustard greens, beets, and other vegetables are grown on the former plantation, along with about two thousand head of cattle and a herd of two hundred ranch horses bred for auction. It's all done with inmate labor, and there's been controversy over that.

We'll come back around to this subject, but first, some more numbers.

Angola's inmate population is about 4,100, down from 6,300 some 10 years ago, but that figure's on the rise again because of Louisiana's worsening crime rates and zero-tolerance sentencing policies. About two-thirds of the inmates are Black and come from broken, dysfunctional families and rough environments. Studies show that most prisoners are incarcerated between the ages of 18 and 25, when they're likeliest to make bad and risky decisions. By the time these young men are psychologically equipped to weigh the consequences of their mistakes, it's often too late, and they've ruined their lives.

Tracy's got all these stats in her head going in. Besides a doctorate in theology, she holds a master's degree in business administration and management, and a bachelor's in ministry leadership. She believes in gathering all the information she can ahead of every situation and then putting it in the hands of the Holy Spirit and asking for insight and illumination. That's to say, she's come spiritually and mentally prepared.

But you can never really prepare for Angola. No matter how much you try, it'll rattle your expectations.

Driving behind Brooks, we pass a sign in the grass—it's really more of a monument—with words credited to a "Bishop" Eugene Tanniehill: *You Are Entering The Land of New Beginnings.* Next to them in two-foot-tall letters: *I've learned to forgive and forget about the things that are behind me. I am pressing forth and reaching for the things that are before me.*

Eugene Tanniehill spent over half a century in Angola for murder and armed robbery. In 1959, he was twenty-four and addicted to drugs and alcohol. One Sunday, strung out for a fix, Tanniehill hid in wait for a preacher he thought would be carrying tithes collected from his congregation. As the preacher walked by the town railroad tracks after services, Tanniehill jumped him from a side road, beat him to death with a pipe, stripped off his clothes looking for the money, then dragged him naked into the weeds. But all he found in the preacher's pocket was $1.63, and he used it to buy half a gallon of wine and "raise some hell."

After his arrest, Tanniehill confessed to killing the man. He was sure he'd get the electric chair for his crime, but didn't care. "I thought I was nothing, never would be nothing, and could be nothing," he said.

If you've been reading this book, you know I once felt exactly like that.

Tanniehill was convicted of first-degree murder and sent to Angola's Death Row. Then one day, after four years in a cell, he heard a voice that he said was a visitation from the Holy Spirit.

"*Tanniehill, who is greater than I?*" it boomed in his ears. According to Tanniehill, the stern voice repeated the question, and then went on to promise that if he repented with godly sorrow his life wouldn't end on the chair.

Tanniehill dropped to his knees and prayed, "I'm a sinner. I done took a man's life. I'm nothing. Will You save me?"

The voice repeated that it would—and that was the beginning of Eugene Tanniehill's redemption and transformation.

That went hand in hand with Angola's transformation under the leadership of its head warden. When Burl Cain took the post in the mid-1990s, the prison was the most violent in the South. Inmates got into knife fights, and he saw blood everywhere. Raised in a town he said was all "pine trees and poor folks," Cain and his family went to a "country church with country values and country preachers." After taking over Angola, Cain looked to his Christian moral teachings to make some decisions.

His biggest was to start a set of faith-based reforms meant to "focus on the soul of the individual" and give inmates "hope where hopelessness reigned."

Eugene Tanniehill was among the first to attend Cain's prison seminary school, become an ordained minister, and go on to teach the Gospel to fellow inmates. Some years later, his death sentence was cut to second-degree murder and life without parole, and in 2007 a review board granted full clemency for the work he'd done to change the prison's culture.

He died a free man in 2020 after spending his last years riding a bike to a steady job, jogging five miles a day, and bringing hope to prisoners around the country with his testimony.

That's why Eugene Tanniehill's words are posted just inside Angola's entrance, where you can hardly miss them. It's no coincidence that what he says about self-forgiveness echoes Paul the Apostle, who writes in Philippians 3:13 about forgetting what is behind and reaching forth toward what lies ahead.

Paul was held by the Romans for two years and often called himself a prisoner.

With the big sign behind us, it's almost like we're driving through a Southern landscape painting: leftover clouds from yesterday's storms, blue sky between them, green pastures and brown dirt farm fields. We pass hundreds of cows, some looking up from their hay to check us out, others grazing too far off to notice us. It's a pretty picture—if not for the fences, razor wire, and sniper towers.

Brooks reaches one of those towers, signals, and turns right toward a low, flat concrete building—its rooftop also strung with wire. I follow her into the parking area out front.

The main prison complex stands against the New Orleans Baptist Theological Seminary, where hundreds of inmates since Eugene Tanniehill became certified pastors. These men do counseling and cell block ministering, notify prisoners of relatives' deaths, officiate inmate funerals, and deliver care packages of snacks, clothing, and personal supplies to those with no money to buy them. They also provide care, comfort, and prayer at the prison treatment center.

Our first stop of the day is its hospice ward, where many inmates spend their last months, weeks, and days on earth.

The saying at Angola goes, "Life means life."

As head warden, Burl Cain knew that with 85 percent of the prisoners being lifers, more would be buried in its cemetery than ever walk out the front gate. When inmates brought him the idea of hospice care to provide comfort and companionship to the dying, it got to his compassionate side. Hundreds of the prisoners had terminal-stage illnesses like hepatitis B, cancer, and AIDS.

Cain wondered about having fellow inmates become caregivers. He never thought of the inmates as bad people—just people who made bad choices, no different at their core from anyone else.

He thought their brainstorm might work. Angola's Bible college was already a success, so why not a volunteer caregiver program? It would give prisoners a chance to help each other. Like his other reforms, it grew out of his small-town upbringing.

Cain found inmate volunteers to get the program off the ground. Though his personal beliefs were rooted in the Gospel of Christ, he was inclusive in pulling men from the general prison population. He found common ground between Christians, Buddhists, and Muslims—and even among groups usually at each other's throats: the Black Panthers and the Aryan Brotherhood.

"All of y'all one day are going to be in hospice," he told them.

Twenty-seven years and two wardens later, Angola's hospice care ward is a model for end-of-life programs in prisons around the country. It has dozens of beds, a nurse, a social worker, and thirty or forty inmate caregivers on rotating shifts.

The hospice is all about giving, and Tracy and I can't wait to do our part as we stand outside with Brooks, waiting for the God Behind Bars team.

They roll up behind Officer Riley's 4x4 after about ten minutes. A half dozen or so young men and women, they're brewing with energy and enthusiasm. One young man strums some chords on an acoustic guitar as he jumps out of their SUV, so I'm guessing he's licked his problem with it.

Riley leads us inside. A few steps past the door, she slows down to talk to a volunteer with a mop in his hand. There's no missing her authority, but I notice how easy and relaxed they are with each other.

Then she turns off the hall to take us into the hospice. The ward's bright with clean white walls and aisle after aisle of hospital beds. Most of the men inside are covered with blankets or sitting in wheelchairs next to IV stands and oxygen machines. Some are watching television sets mounted high up near the ceiling. A few patients sit up in bed to get a look at us. Others are asleep or too weak to raise their heads.

"This section's palliative care," a nurse explains. She says it in a low voice and waits to make sure we understand.

Palliative care is about making people comfortable when they're reaching the end of their lives. I remember when my mother could no longer tolerate the radiation treatments she was getting for her cancer. By then she knew it couldn't be cured. The treatments might have slowed it down, but she used to say they made her sicker than the disease.

Finally, she decided enough was enough, and was placed in palliative care in those final days.

Knowing some of the men are days, or even hours, from their last breath, and seeing their drawn faces, I can understand someone thinking this would be a grim experience. But my heart attack reminded me the clock's ticking for everybody. It was a lesson I'll never forget. No one knows when theirs will stop; we all need to consider how we're going to use the time we have. Accepting that it's going to run out someday is a giant step to maturity.

I can't heal the inmates' bodies. I can't change their outward circumstances. But I can step in and show them a path toward spiritual healing. As a minister, I've come to pray for them, give them comfort and hope, and let them know it isn't too late to get right with themselves and God.

It starts by telling them they aren't alone. Not all the men in the ward understand how sick they are. Not all of them know they're dying. But I can see the loneliness in their sunken eyes. The fear. The questions about what's ahead.

They're questions we all ask sooner or later.

I am pressing forth and reaching for the things that are before me.

I haven't come to pass out answers like gift coupons. All I can do is show these men a path so they can find those answers for themselves.

"That fella—he played football, right?"

"Baseball."

"What's his name?"

"Darryl Strawberry."

"Strawberry? Thought he was with the Raiders. Or was it the Falcons? Man could bust it."

"Actually, he was with the Mets and Yankees. Well, mostly. Like I said, he played baseball . . . "

"What position?"

"Right field. Anyway, he's a minister now. That's why he's here. Would you like to speak with him?"

"Yes, sir. I would. But you sure he didn't play football?"

I'll hear about this conversation between a patient and one of the GBB team afterward. Right now I'm focused on my work, offering each inmate I pass a smile and a hello. Some give me stony looks. Some turn away or pretend they're asleep. But they're exceptions. I can tell when someone's glad to see visitors, and they usually are. There's a look on a man's face, something in his eyes that tells me he's longing for some greater connection—words of encouragement, a human touch, a prayer. I pay attention to those faces as I move from bed to bed.

James is thin and frail as a sick bird. He has a gray beard and light brown skin with a pale yellow tone that can't mean anything good. He says he feels okay but is unable to keep down solid food. How long's that been going on? Six months, maybe closer to a year—he doesn't remember. James claims he's getting better little by little, sounding like he doesn't believe it.

He says he'd like to eat more than a few spoonfuls of oatmeal at a time, if only the reflux would stop burning his insides.

James is one of several men who don't seem to grasp how sick they are. The social workers and nurses try to prepare them, so they can think about their last wishes and make arrangements with their people on the outside—if they have people. But not all of them understand the medical information, and some are probably in denial . . . or can't face up to it because of the load of guilt and regret they're carrying.

There's a look of fear in their eyes, I see it over and over. They haven't forgiven themselves for the things they've done and don't really expect God to forgive them when the time comes.

James has that same scared look. After we share a few words—I finally convince him I'm not Eric Dickerson without goggles—I ask if he'd like a prayer, and he nods.

I sit down at the edge of his bed, take his hand into both of mine, close my eyes, and pray for his physical and spiritual healing. The Bible teaches us about the hope of glory, and though Tracy's got the doctor's degree and can explain its meaning better than I know how, it boils down to the promise of God's salvation being in all of us. I always say Christ shed His holy blood to fulfill that promise on our behalf. That we only need to open our heart to His love and guidance, and that to do so is to receive the grace of His redemption.

James leans his head against my arm and prays along with me—I feel the power of it flowing through the warmth of our clasped hands. I bow my head and pray our Father will strengthen him, heal him, and give him courage to face up to whatever he needs to face up to. When the supernatural power of Christ comes into a man, it cleanses and purifies him, and I pray James will find the words to invite it into every aspect of his life.

I don't count the minutes I spend with him, but it feels like we're together longer than is really possible. Riley and Brooks are sticking to the schedule, and I have limited time to stop at the ward's remaining beds. When we've completed our prayers, I put my arms around James, give him a hug, and pull his blankets up over his bony shoulders.

I don't know that Tracy's been watching us, and I won't until she brings it up later that night . . . and then blows me away by revealing why. But I'll get to that in the next chapter.

As I pass through the ward, I see an inmate who's so weak he can't move at all. He's lying on his back, the bed slightly elevated, his head propped on a couple of pillows. A gray knit cap is drawn down over his forehead and his blanket's pulled up to his chin.

There's nothing fleshy or heavy about his face or neck, and I don't think he's normally overweight. But his stomach's unnaturally swollen under the blanket, like something's grown inside him that shouldn't be there.

I get up close to his bed rail and ask his name.

He doesn't answer. I'm not sure he has enough breath to answer. But his eyes say he wants me to stay a bit.

In them, I recognize the guys I knew growing up in South Central—caught up in gangs, crap games, and all the bad stuff on the street. I see so many of us, fatherless and feeling crushed by life. And I see myself as a younger man, trying to drown my childhood hurts with drugs, drinking, sex, and chasing material things.

I can also see that he's probably on his deathbed. My focus can't be on the prisoner of the correctional system, but on the prisoner inside him—a hostage to pain that needs to be set free.

The ward's busy and noisy. I hear medical carts rolling over the concrete floor, televisions, and the GBB team circulating around the room doing what they do best—giving love to the sickest, brightening their day with a song or just some kind words. The inmates who are able to get around are talking to caregivers and each other, playing chess, or just having something to eat at a table.

This adds up to a big racket. But I've learned a great deal from Trace, including the power of stillness in a noisy world. It was in solitude, with my phone off, a Bible in my hands, and my face in God's Word, that I found His most profound teaching.

As a ballplayer, I made my quiet space the batter's box. I didn't think of it that way at the time, but that's what it was. Now I bring my quiet space with me wherever I go.

I lean in close to the man and speak softly, bringing him into that place with me. I want him to know I've gone through my own struggles and been in my own dark valleys. I want him to understand I'm not going to judge him. And I want him to see he's reached a point in his life when he can no longer lean on his worldly understanding, but has to find something deeper.

I've heard people talk about leaps of faith, but to me it's more about acceptance and surrender, an acknowledgment that we're putting our trust in the Lord. It's opening a door in our hearts to release our hurts and receiving His grace through that same open door.

When I preach, I talk about how Hebrews 11:1 defines faith as "the substance of things hoped for, the evidence of things not seen." If his heart's beating, this man can open it to the evidence of things not seen. When I learned that, it transformed me, and it can transform him.

He still has time to change. That's really the simple message I leave with him. He still has time, if he'll allow himself the faith.

My words aren't perfect like the biblical verse, but suddenly the man's eyes are wet. I see a teardrop spill from one of them and reach down to lay a hand over his cap.

"You're gonna be all right," I tell my wounded brother. "You got this, okay? You got it."

I remember him giving me the tiniest of nods, and know the effort it must have taken. When he does that, I pump my fist, give him an "Amen" . . . and he somehow gathers up the strength to answer.

I read his lips more than hear it. But that's enough for me.

What he says is, "Amen."

People think "Death Row" is prison slang, tough talk for the place where condemned men wait to die.

Not so.

At maximum-security penitentiaries in death penalty states, it's a literal place. Like a street sign on the corner of Main Street, the sign marking Death Row doesn't leave any doubt where you are.

Angola's Death Row is in one of several outcamp buildings, set apart from the main prison complex. We trail Riley and Brooks in our SUVs, heading out through another stretch of weird beauty—horse corrals, crop fields, ducks drifting in slow backwaters.

After about a mile, we pull off into a small parking area for a quick orientation. Outside our vehicles, Riley, the senior officer, tells us we'll have to leave everything we came with in the SUVs—our phones, purses, man packs . . . I can't even bring the dog-eared old Bible I usually take everywhere.

She explains that we've come at a somber time for the inmates. Just three weeks before our visit, the state carried out its first execution in fifteen years. Louisiana's new governor, we're told, ended the long pause soon after taking office. The executed man, Jessie Hoffman Jr., was forty-six. He'd been convicted of the brutal abduction, rape, and murder of a woman when he was only eighteen.

I wasn't surprised to learn his violence was rooted in a cycle of abuse and neglect. Family members said he was hogtied and tortured by his father as a child for not knowing his ABCs. His mother, who was sexually abusive, whipped him with belts and extension cords and forced him to hold his hands over the flame on a kitchen stove until they blistered. If she didn't see blisters, she made him put them back over the fire. He still had burn scars on his hands when prison guards escorted him to the execution chamber.

The social worker assigned to his case said she never knew anyone who'd endured more severe childhood trauma.

Jessie Hoffman chose his victim at random: a twenty-eight-year-old woman who left her car in the parking garage where he worked as a valet. Her loss devastated her loved ones and traumatized them forever.

I can't imagine how I'd feel if she were my wife or daughter—"shattered" wouldn't describe it. She had her whole life ahead of her and someone took it away. But if we're ever going to prevent such horrendous crimes, we need to get to their root cause.

This cycle of pain reminds me of a verse from the Old Testament (Hosea 8:7): "*For they have sown the wind, and they shall reap the whirlwind.*"

I'm no weather scientist, but I know a tornado—or whirlwind—forms when air currents spin inside a thundercloud, feeding on its energy. The more air it pulls in, the faster and more dangerous it becomes, drawing in everything nearby. There's just darkness and cold emptiness inside the roaring wind.

Tornadoes can uproot fifty-foot trees and tear through entire blocks of houses when they touch down. We've had our share in the St. Louis area, and I've seen the destruction they leave behind. There's a warning system in place—sirens, alerts for people to evacuate or take shelter in basements. But everyone doesn't respond in time, and the system's been known to fail.

Think of abuse as being like a thundercloud that creates an emptiness inside its victims and churns up unbearable pain around it. Unless they come to terms with that pain and let it go, they eventually spin out of control.

When that happens, we all suffer as a society.

Riley tells us that Jessie Hoffman became a profoundly changed man over his three decades of imprisonment—deeply remorseful and a mentor to others. Until just days before his execution, he continued to lead Alcoholics Anonymous and Narcotics Anonymous groups and facilitated faith-based roundtables with interdenominational Christian ministers.

As she talks about all this, Riley can't hide her sadness. She knows the men on Death Row committed terrible crimes. She doesn't make excuses for them. But she explains that prosecutors often decide whether to seek life imprisonment or the death penalty based on things other than the nature of a crime: politics, publicity, even whether they like the defendant's personality. That's just how the system works.

Riley's thinking out loud, and I can tell she's trying to square it all away in her own mind and heart. It isn't easy when we look at the system's unfairness. But I believe *God's* system works way past such factors. He capitalizes on our gravest sins, forcing the sinner to take a profound look into the same emptiness that provoked the sin itself. He brings a deep sorrow, a remorseful reflection that only the Holy Spirit can make flourish inside us. It can take days, months, years . . . or come in a minute. But when it happens, it's like receiving a bouquet of flowers, fresh and blooming with life.

"I think it's good the men are getting visitors right now," Riley says. "They need a pick-me-up."

We ride in two 4x4 prison transport vehicles—Trace and I with Brooks and some of the God Behind Bars team, Riley driving the rest. Also with her group are three trustee photographers and video camera operators, covering our visit for Angola's news magazine and LSP-TV, the prison's inmate-run television station. At a checkpoint, the 4x4 stops and lifts for an undercarriage scan. Then we pass through a gate, it closes behind us, and we leave the transports.

Escorted into Death Row, we pass a wall with color photos of all its inmates. Fifty-five, total. That's one less than there was a few weeks before.

Then something else on the wall catches my eye—a framed painting that stretches almost from floor to ceiling. The main figure's a man in a chariot, with long white hair and a white beard, dressed in flowing white robes. The chariot rises into the sky, pulled by two flaming white horses beneath a dark, stormy sky.

The man holds the horses' reins while looking back over his shoulder at a second man on the ground, at the water's edge. He has a short, black beard and shaved head and wears a humble sackcloth frock. A white cloth is falling through the storm between the two figures.

I realize this is the moment when the Lord brings the prophet Elijah up to heaven in a whirlwind. The white cloth is his mantle, and he's cast it down to his disciple Elisha, who stands waiting on the bank of the river Jordan.

He took up Elijah's cloak that had fallen from him.

In biblical times, the cloak signified divine authority. Elijah's successor was chosen not by Elijah himself, but through God's will. He has a plan for all of us, even if we can't see it.

The painting's beautiful, and I know an inmate painted it without having to ask. It's a scene Burl Cain and Eugene Tanniehill would appreciate—and one that leaves me with something to think about.

As I walk to the cell block, it hits: The whirlwind, with all the pain and chaos that comes with it, is also God's will—part of His master plan—and He uses it to shape us in ways that are beyond our understanding.

We're on Death Row with the inmates for over an hour. The cells are arranged in tiers, one man to a cell. Each measures 6' x 9'—about the size of a walk-in closet. Inside's a steel sink, steel toilet, footlocker, a slab bed, and a small steel shelf bolted to the wall. The cells have concrete ceilings, concrete floors, and concrete-block walls on three sides.

The inmates were told we were coming in advance, and they're allowed to stand in their open cell doors and talk. But they keep their toes behind an invisible line, just outside the walkway. They don't need to look down at their feet to know they're on the right side of that line. Prison's taught them to feel it without checking.

I can't compare ministering on Death Row to anything else I've done. It's a profound and rewarding experience, but there's a weight to it.

Most inmates at Angola will never leave. I know that. But I understand that, however he wound up there, whether his sentence is life or capital punishment, the most important decision a man has to make is how he'll manage the remainder of his days on earth.

Will he trust himself enough to grow and become a different person? Trust a higher power to give him the necessary strength? He can't choose to do what he wants with his time. He has to do what he's told according to the prison's routines. But one thing he *can do* is ask himself those questions.

Men sentenced to capital punishment face the same questions as the rest of the inmates, but they're carrying an added load. Each of them knows the day will probably come when a judge signs a warrant for his execution. When his time will run out.

Death Row inmates don't get many visitors. They're only allowed to gather with men on their own tier, placing them in even deeper isolation than other prisoners. Some are only in their thirties, forties, or fifties, and most are in good health—the institution provides solid medical care. But they live waiting for the court to set their end date.

Unlike the men in hospice, they'll be put to death as healthy individuals who might otherwise have years, or decades, ahead of them. As someone stepping into their world, it gives you a different kind of feeling.

Life puts traps in front of us. Greed, envy, ego, lust . . . they've always existed, and always will. Whatever the inmates of Death Row did to put themselves where they are—whatever traps they fell into—I'm not here to snap my fingers and get them out. I don't go to Death Row thinking I have the power to save them. I go there knowing what walking the spiritual walk can do to save them, and wanting to show them that path is right there for them.

No matter the things they've done, I truly believe they all have enough good inside to give to somebody else and love on other people. And it can start with them accepting it from us.

We say hello, shake their hands, hug them, and get big, warm bear hugs right back. We listen as they talk about themselves, sharing their hopes and fears, and we pray with them if they're open to it. Mostly, we offer love and compassion, and let them know we see them as people—not just inmates. Not as mistakes. They've made mistakes, but God doesn't make mistakes. God makes all His children in His image. That can't be a mistake by definition.

They're men, brothers, souls. Seen, heard, felt, and alive.

Even on Death Row, alive.

Ahead of our service, we spend a few hours touring the camps outside the main prison complex. The men wear gray or white T-shirts with jeans or sweatpants, more practical and functional for a Southern work camp than stiff, standard issue coveralls. I'm in jeans and a gray hoodie that fit right in, partly to remind myself I'm no better than they are, and partly to let them know.

I just learned some hard lessons, and made better choices over time. But I was once prisoner number T17169 at Gainesville Correctional in Florida. When you fall, you don't know how deep it will be. I easily could have wound up in a place like this.

In one dorm, the men are under lockdown and confined to their beds, usually punishment for contraband, fights, or disobedience. When one messes up, the whole dorm pays.

The air's thick. Nobody talks much. Losing privileges hits hard when there are so few to start. Some of the men sit quietly, writing on yellow legal pads or reviewing parole packets and clemency petitions. Fewer than 1 percent at Angola get clemency each year, but hope keeps them going—a chance for life beyond these walls.

Riley says most prisoners in the outcamps will attend services tonight. Even the ones in lockdown will get supervised chapel privileges if they weren't involved in whatever happened.

Tracy and I walk the rows inviting men to hear our testimony. A Muslim prison leader says he'll bring a group, and I think it's great. I'm not telling anyone how to pray, or asking anyone to share my faith. I just want to open hearts.

I lose count of how many we talk to in dorms, in the yard during exercise, or tossing scraps to half-wild cats—there's a colony around the camp, dozens of them, most outside the fences. They look suspicious and never get too close. When one on our side of the fence rubs up against my leg, a prisoner grabs my arm to stop me from petting him.

"We call him Scratchy," he says. "You don't want to find out why."

By late afternoon, we're at the chapel. Trustees set up musical instruments, microphones, and mixing boards, and they're as professional as any top sound crew. I'm ready to rock, but first . . .

"Can I get my Bible out of my SUV now?" I ask Riley.

She smiles and nods toward her transport. "I'll give you a lift back to where you're parked."

About two hours later, I'm in the prison chapel, listening to Tracy give her testimony to the gathered men. I'll be up next to preach—but right now, I'm just another member of the congregation.

They, *we*, all two hundred of us, hang on to her every word.

"I was out there for a long time," Tracy says into the microphone. "And I didn't want to be that person."

She doesn't stand behind the pulpit. She stands in front of the stage, down in the aisle, close to the inmates in the first pew. It's the same when she worships. She's always at the front of the congregation, her hands open to receive the Holy Spirit, like cups waiting to be filled.

Out there for a long time. They know what she means—they've been out there too.

"There are things that were done to you, done to me, that none of us asked for. That we didn't sign up for. What do you do with all that?"

She doesn't go into the abuse she suffered from a neighbor as a young girl, or the addictions she turned to just to bury the pain. They don't need to hear the details. Most of these men have lived through abuse—and all have caused harm to others. In cycles like these, roles blur. The abused becomes the abuser.

"It's torment," she says. "You were imprisoned before you ever ended up here. Prisoners of your heart, prisoners of your mind. How many of you know it?"

Tracy puts her hand in the air. A second later, they go up all around the prison chapel.

"Day in, day out, I let my pain reign over my life and guide my choices," she says. "Anger, rage, impulsive behavior—I made decisions I never thought I would, did things I never thought I'd do. And when a woman's doing these things, there's another stigma . . ."

Tracy was clean and sober for almost two years when her ex-husband sued for custody of their three sons. She'd gotten baptized, and was in discipleship studying the Gospel. But her lawyer advised that her past mistakes would compromise her to the court—and that the boys might end up in foster care if she contested their father's legal action. She couldn't put them through that. So, for their sake, she let them go.

"But I knew there was still breath in my body," she tells the men. "My kids needed me to show up and be the mom that God created me to be, whether or not I would see them again."

The room's still. They're listening, really feeling her. These men are violent offenders. They've been convicted of the worst kinds of crimes. And they realize this slight, well put-together woman from outside cares enough about them to open her restored heart—and show them theirs can be healed too.

Tracy tells them she wrote her sons letters. She wanted them to know how much she loved them, and how sorry she was for what she'd put them through. But she knew it wasn't enough just to be sorry, or promise she'd change. She would have to show them.

She wrote those letters almost every day, asking for forgiveness. But she didn't drop a *single one of them in the mail.* Instead, she kept them in boxes, storing them away until she felt she'd earned her children's trust.

It would be a ten-year journey. Ten years before she felt she was ready.

To this day, I can't imagine how hard it must have been for her. But she was determined not to let them down again. And to her that meant standing up and becoming the woman and mother she needed to be.

Tracy talks about the work she did to make herself into that woman. She talks about asking God's forgiveness, and her children's forgiveness, knowing it wouldn't take away the pain she caused them and make everything okay. She talks about rebuilding lost trust with actions, step by step, until it became a bridge between them.

And finally, she says, the letters were all read, and the relationship with her sons began to mend.

Today they're as close as any family can be.

As the men rise to their feet with tears in their eyes, I try not to be too much the proud husband. I'm a minister, and I've come to preach. But even after twenty years of marriage, knowing how things turned out, her courage and honesty humble me.

I stand up and clap with the rest.

"Memories are powerful," she says. "I'm praying God heals your memories. I'm praying God *heals you.* Because if you let Him, He'll deliver you. But you have to decide pain won't run your lives anymore."

We're all still out of our chairs. Finished giving testimony, Tracy tells the men she's God's setup for me, and explains that I'm going to bring them the Word. But *setup* doesn't really cover what she's done. For me, she's the main act. I'll be the one delivering the sermon, but she's prepared the ground, laying the promise of restoration right at their feet.

I wait for the cheers to quiet down and carry my Bible up to the stage.

Sometimes you look into people's eyes and see their hearts—and sometimes, when you touch their hearts, you can feel their souls.

It isn't easy for me to find words for the joy I get from preaching to incarcerated men and women. People on the outside like to tell themselves they've got it all together. That's as true for me as anyone else. Getting comfortable in our daily existence is human nature.

But none of us have everything figured out. None of us is fully in control of our lives. We're all day-to-day, even if we don't think about it. Our lives can change at any second.

My heart attack drove that home for me.

Those behind prison walls and fences can't pretend everything's fine, not in the way we often do. They don't have that luxury. When I visit with them, their welcome's emotionally raw. Gratitude pours out of them. They aren't used to having anyone take the time out of their day to see them, shake their hands, and give them a hug. To say hello, ask their names, and walk in the yard alongside them.

When they're in chapel, they worship full on. They aren't concerned with being proper or polite—they just let it all out, raw and unfiltered. They hardly ever stay seated. They raise their hands in the air, sing their praises of the Lord, and dance and sway in the aisles. They give themselves up to the moment without worrying how it'll look to anyone.

To me, that's holy. Holy singing from deep down in the spirit. Holy surrender to God.

For a minute after Tracy's testimony, the men sit down to catch their breath. But before I take the pulpit, the praise band brings them back to their feet. I recognize faces from throughout the day. From every camp, every dormitory, even hospice care.

I see one ancient-looking man in a wheelchair with a blanket over his legs and a homemade knitted cap on his head. Though he has trouble sitting up straight, he's singing with everything in him.

As they rise, I rise. Physically and spiritually, singing along in my off-key tuba voice. I'm really feeling it, like a wave's washing over and through me.

Jesus is one bad dude, I think—and maybe even say it aloud when the music lowers.

I stand looking over the congregation. I'm there so the men will know someone cares about them, to give them hope, and to help them see it's never too late for a new direction, a new start at an abundant life.

You could count them as three separate goals, but I'd sum them up this way: *I've come to set these brothers free.*

Before sharing the Word, I let them know I understand being behind bars—because I've been there. T17169. That was me. But I believe God was at work in putting me there. If He hadn't stopped me from using at that time, doing what I couldn't do for myself, I probably would have died on the street or in a crack house.

God sometimes *has* to bring you to a full STOP. And one thing I know is that He's in the business of completion. He can bring you from nowhere to somewhere. Like I always say, He brought me from the pit to the pulpit.

All these men have life and breath. That means all of them still have a chance, like Tracy and I did when we were lost. I want them to recognize that no matter what they've been through, God still has purpose for their lives.

As it says in Ephesians 3:20, "Now to Him who is able to do exceedingly abundantly above all that we ask or think, according to the power that works in us."

To me, that means God can do so much more than we ask or even imagine—He never falls short. He knows *we* fall short, and that's what makes His love so powerful. His power is limitless, and His wonderful, working presence is alive in each of us. Our flesh tells us do this, do that, but we just have to tell it to shut up and let our Spirit Man work. We just have to say yes to Him. Because we can't do it on our own.

"And you know what happened to me?" I ask the men. I can feel them like we're all one, totally united in that chapel. "Ever since I allowed my Spirit Man to work, I've never been in handcuffs again. Because I love when the Spirit works. The Spirit is there for love, peace, joy, wisdom, knowledge . . . The Spirit is there to help us navigate through this life."

Out of the corner of my eye, I see Riley gesturing at me. I've done prison ministry for years, and I won't say that her signal intrudes. The light's gotten dim outside the chapel windows, and it's almost time for the count, when the men are confined for the night.

I call them forward, and they come close, hands laying on—three, four, five deep. We're like a charging battery: energy flowing through us, the Spirit moving in us, filling all of us.

A young man steps up, and my hand finds his chest. I don't know what he did to land in a maximum-security prison. But when I look into his eyes, I see his heart. And touching his heart, I feel his soul.

And I love him for the soul God created.

I let him, and all of them, know that the ground they stand on is sacred ground. Sacred ground isn't on the outside, and it isn't in the prison either. Christ shed His blood for them, and by accepting Him, they make it sacred wherever they walk, wherever they stand.

I conclude with a prayer:

"We thank You, Father, for allowing us to come in here to speak life into these brothers and show them the love of God.

May they receive what You have spoken into their lives tonight.

May lives be transformed.

May they challenge themselves, continue to push themselves, to look up to You and say:

'God, help me. I need Your strength. I need Your comfort and love.

Help me become better.

Help me to speak in a different vocabulary.

Help me trust You, even when I don't know how to trust.'

And, Father, may they walk in a new season—with faith and not with doubt or fear.

May they go back to their beds tonight and meditate on You—on who You are, and what You have spoken into their hearts this evening.

Your Word is powerful, Lord. It breaks chains, renews minds, and restores lives.

We thank You, and we give You all the honor and the glory.

In Jesus's name we pray,

Amen."

Chapter Eight

That Old Me Is Behind Me

It's ten o'clock at night, and we're in Baton Rouge again, grabbing something to eat at one of those fast-food melted sandwich joints, one of the few places near the hotel still open after a long, slow drive from Angola through the pitch dark. Across the table, Trace is inhaling a chicken-jalapeño wrap that's gooey with melted cheese. I'm trying to put my appetite to bed with a cheesesteak sandwich and fries. I don't eat like that often after my heart attack. But every now and then, when preaching's worked up a hunger as big as a whale's and there's nowhere else to eat, I ease up on the rules.

We'll worry about upset stomachs in the morning.

"You know that picture of you and your dad?" Tracy asks.

The question's a surprise. But I know the one she means.

"At the hospital?"

"Yes. Do you have it?"

“I don’t think it’s on my phone. But I bet Ronnie does. Want me to find out?”

“Please.”

I call my brother. California’s two hours behind us, so it’s only eight o’clock there. Sure enough, he has it.

I ask him to text it to me.

Ron took the picture six months before our father passed, when we visited him for the last time. It shows me leaning over Dad’s bedside and smiling at the camera lens, my arm resting on his pillow. He’s in a johnny, with a blanket tucked around his waist. You can see how weak he is—he’s almost a skeleton, his eyes barely open. A monitor cable’s clipped to the side of the bed.

I remember being in San Diego to preach at a men’s conference when Ron called. He said Dad had a stroke and might be near the end. The hospital wasn’t far from the conference, but I fought the idea of visiting him.

I called Tracy from my hotel, gave her the news, and told her I wasn’t going.

She said she felt I had to.

I repeated that I wouldn’t. But I’d called her for a reason. I didn’t want to admit it, but I wanted her to plant a seed of doubt in me.

She told me again that I needed to go. I knew she would, of course.

I kept resisting her. After all the things he’d done to our family—his drinking and nights at the racetrack, his physical and verbal abuse—the hurt went too deep. I didn’t think I could find the forgiveness.

I thought back to the times I would be coming home from school and just walk on past our house because I knew Dad was there ready to beat on me. I thought of the times he’d play weekend baseball with his team from the post office, send my mother home after the game, and head right over to a bar for hours, sometimes taking me and Ronnie along. Sometimes picking up other women.

I’ve never told anyone, but back when I was a player, I would imagine that every swing I took was at my father's head. I didn't know what to do with my anger, so I brought it onto the field and made it part of my game. Once, I crushed a ball that hit the roof of Olympic Stadium in Montreal. The world never knew it was really Henry Strawberry's head. If the roof at the Big O hadn't stopped it, that homer might have traveled 550 feet.

I didn't want to see him.

But then God spoke to me at the hotel. It was a true visitation—I heard His voice in my head and He wasn't pleased. Word for word, he said, "How dare you not forgive him when I forgave you and gave you grace."

That did it—I was outnumbered. You could say Tracy had one powerful ally in the Man Upstairs. But deep down I knew she'd been right all along. I'd struggled for years not offering Henry the same grace of forgiveness Christ *gave me*. Though I didn't deserve it, He gave it to me anyway. Yet here I was, still a captive of my own painful emotions, and getting ready to testify to a large group of men about the freedom to be found in that grace.

I'd let those emotions build a wall around me. If I wanted to break through it, I would need to walk the walk.

I drove to the hospital thinking I would let go of the past. Forgive Henry for all the cruelty and misery he'd heaped on my family, his total neglect of his role as a husband and father figure. It wouldn't be easy. He'd once had a chance to earn that forgiveness and rejected it.

In 1994, just before I signed midseason with the Giants, I spent a month at Betty Ford trying to get clean. At the suggestion of my counselors, I asked Henry to visit. I was hoping he would finally own up to his behavior, but he denied everything: the drinking, the violence, the abandonment. I remembered him being more honest in a newspaper interview, where he admitted to his gambling even as he shrugged off how much it hurt my mother.

"If you don't take gambling, you don't take me," he said. "It's a part of my life."

As selfish and unconcerned as that was, my father had given the reporter more truth than he gave me at Betty Ford, even if that would have helped with my rehabilitation. His refusal to admit to anything he'd done didn't just reopen old wounds in my heart—it carved a new one.

But there's no testimony without a test. It didn't matter whether or not Henry deserved my forgiveness—or anyone's. I didn't deserve it when I was saved, but God gave it to me anyway.

I had to allow Henry that same grace. It would be the biggest test of my life—harder than overcoming cancer and drug addiction, harder than spending almost a year in jail. But I couldn't let my emotions steer me in the wrong direction. In spite of everything, I had to go to the hospital and offer him my forgiveness.

In the years since Betty Ford, I had studied the Bible and been transformed. I'd learned some things—about myself, about God's purpose for me . . . and about my father's past. A relative told me Henry had been abused by his own father, and that his mother—my grandmother—was also mistreated. I've said many times that no one in my life hurt me more than my father. And then I'd found out Henry had as much harm done to him as he'd done to others, and could never face it head-on. It left him trapped in a generational cycle of verbal abuse and physical violence.

I *had* faced it—all of it. With the Lord's help, I'd broken the cycle he couldn't. But even though I realized Dad was in pain, I'd never let him into my world. Never sent him tickets to see me play at the ballpark or get together with his grandkids.

Knowing he was a prisoner of that pain, I wished I had tried harder.

As I headed over to see him, I finally knew what I needed to do—and it wasn't what I expected leaving my hotel.

The Holy Spirit had guided me toward Henry's bedside. The rest was on me.

At the hospital, I asked my father a question I hadn't expected would ever leave my mouth.

"Dad, will you forgive me?"

The miracle that day—the true miracle—was that he said yes. When the word escaped him, I saw a single teardrop spill from his eye and down his cheek. And then I broke down into tears of my own. They blurred my vision as I fell across Dad's lap, my chest hitching with sobs as I told him how sorry I was for keeping him at a distance.

For a while I just stayed there with my throat clogged, crying so hard I could hardly breathe. It felt like there would be no end to the tears. They just kept pouring out of me. I remember looking up and seeing Ron crying too.

I eventually pulled myself together enough to tell Dad how Christ had changed my life by forgiving my sins. Then I surprised myself by asking if he wanted to experience that same forgiveness.

I didn't remember him being a man of faith. But he nodded that he did.

I led him in the Sinner's Prayer, bringing him to the Lord, and afterward noticed he was getting tired. Ronnie and I said goodbye and left.

I didn't think I'd ever see him again, and I was right.

Six months later, he was gone from this earth.

But when I left his hospital room, I was free. Truly free for the first time in my life. The pain I'd carried around like a hundred-ton boulder was gone. The weight was lifted off my shoulders. I believe it was the same for Dad.

That day will always be clear in my mind, standing as a powerful example of what restoration is about. In our shared forgiveness, we created a circle of healing around us.

I think sometimes we don't fully understand that a key part of God's grace is that He gives it to us even when we don't deserve it. The Lord wanted to give it to my father without being concerned with whether he'd earned it or not. He used me to extend the very grace I'd received.

All this runs through my head at the restaurant as I show Tracy the photo. It feels like yesterday that my brother snapped it.

She studies it, then scrolls on her phone, and without a word holds it up to show me a different snapshot. It's from that morning at Angola, taken in the hospice. I'm with James—the inmate who thought I played football—sitting on the edge of his bed. His head's on my shoulder as we pray together.

Take a few years off my face, and it could be me and my father.

I study it for a few seconds, then look across at Trace and remember her testimony: *To experience the power of forgiveness is to become different . . . And that old me is behind me.*

"Talk about full circle," she says, like she'd been reading my mind. "Huh, honey?"

I smile at her. She smiles back.

Then we put away our phones and get back to our greasy, high-calorie, delicious guilty pleasure sandwiches, finishing up without another word.

Chapter Nine

Ordinary Heroes

I'm going to introduce you to some superheroes.

Okay, you got me. I've never seen any of them fly or lift a house over their heads, so I don't think they'd mind if we just called them "heroes" and left it right there. In fact, I suspect they'd prefer to be known as ordinary people who believe in the superpower of community.

We'll start with the heroes of Saugerties, New York.

I met them in the summer of 2018, when I was invited to speak at the local high school by a group called RYAN. It was founded by Carole and Vincent Kelder in memory of their late son, Ryan, who struggled with drug addiction for years and died of an overdose just short of his twenty-fifth birthday.

RYAN, the organization, stands for Raising Your Awareness about Narcotics. The Kelders and their daughter, Randi, launched its first annual event two months after Ryan's passing in 2015. They set high goals—and when I say they're willing to knock down walls to make them happen, I mean that literally. Vince is always about ten minutes away from grabbing a hammer and table saw to help their latest, most large-scale project become real.

HOPE Rocks is another group of Saugerties heroes. Joe Defino, who started it up, tells you its mission is "restoring hope to those who struggle with depression, addiction, and social isolation."

Joe's a former elementary school teacher, with silver hair, glasses, and a friendly, average-guy way about him. There's a depth to him, a kind of humility that brings out the best in people.

Joe says all his years as an educator gave him a good read on young people, and some of the things he noticed got to him. He remembers seeing kindergarten kids step off the school bus carrying emotional baggage they couldn't put into words. He saw it in their eyes, and in the way they carried themselves. Even as five-year-olds, they seemed to be under a cloud. He'd learn over time that the causes of their troubles were as different and unique as the kids themselves.

In those days, he had his hands full with the everyday duties of teaching—lesson plans, homework, grading test papers. He also had his responsibilities as a husband and father. He was limited in how much he could influence his students after school.

Then drugs started taking a toll on the kids who passed through his classroom.

By 2016, he'd gone to eight former students' funerals—students who died from suicide or overdose. Over the next couple of years, five more were lost, bringing the number of casualties to thirteen.

Thirteen young lives, cut short. Losing that many kids in a small community is hard for any of us to imagine, yet at the same time we know it's happening all around the country. It was a tragedy Joe couldn't stand by and accept.

That first time I came to Saugerties for RYAN, one of two high school students who interviewed me on internet TV was a young man named Kieran Defino. The second name's no coincidence. Kieran is Joe's son (he's also a Mets fan, so he scores extra points). But RYAN and HOPE Rocks are linked by more than the webcast's cohost.

Joe and the Kelders see each other often to talk about community efforts. They've been working together since 2017—the same year Joe says an alarm went off in his head about the chaos drugs and suicide were causing for young people and their families.

At the time, Carole Kelder was the principal at another school in Joe's district. Joe knew about her son Ryan's overdose and the organization her family had started in his memory. He brought an idea to her and a representative of the American Foundation for Suicide Prevention for a new kind of program.

Both women were a hundred percent on board, and that program became HOPE Rocks.

Joe and Carole will tell you their groups are fighting the same battle, just from different angles. RYAN House gives young people with substance and emotional struggles a place to meet, get counseling, and work things out in an environment that feels safe. HOPE Rocks puts on events like music festivals and sports tournaments that connect (there's that word again) people with sponsors and charities that want to help.

That's networking aimed at saving lives, not building up careers.

It helps to think of addiction as a disease. Say you get a bad virus. Your doctor might prescribe medication to treat it. A nutritionist may recommend food and vitamins to help your immune system fight it off. A fitness instructor will have a plan to build your physical strength through exercise. If it's a lasting illness, or one that leaves psychological or emotional effects, counseling or therapy makes sense.

Any one of these can help you get better. But if you view the parts of what's making you sick as connected, and take an all-around approach to wellness, you'll heal faster—and be healthier overall. That's the idea behind holistic medicine, and I guess you could say this is a holistic approach to recovery.

Joe would say it's about using the full set of tools, and faith-based support is one of the tools available. We need to fight addiction with everything in the kit.

The opioid epidemic spreading through America is the most heartbreaking thing I've ever seen. Drugs find their way into every neighborhood and schoolyard. Rich, poor, Black, white—whatever our family's race or economic status, we're all vulnerable.

Epidemic. Think of that word.

Addiction is a disease.

I've come to Saugerties to do my part in fighting it by attending a high school baseball tournament, talking to the players about my experiences with drugs and alcohol, and passing on the spiritual tools that helped me.

With me are my son Jordan and Minister John Luppo, whom you last saw with me in Las Vegas. I arrived earlier that day at LaGuardia Airport in Queens, New York, and Jordan and I made the hundred-mile drive from there. John flew to Albany from his home in Florida, and we met in the middle at a hotel that was a paper mill a long time ago.

Saugerties used to be one of the country's leading papermaking towns. If you lived there fifty or a hundred years ago, you or someone in your family probably worked at one of the mills.

Nothing ever replaced the industry when it went down in the late 1970s, and these days Saugerties is like any number of places I visit in my travels—good, steady jobs hard to find, its young people seeing no future in the area, and not knowing how they can earn enough to make futures for themselves anywhere else. Even close to New York City, a lot of middle-class Saugerties kids must feel life there's out of reach. All they need to do is check out the expensive apartment rental listings.

The Friday night we arrive in town, I'm chaufeuring Jordan and John back from dinner with our hosts when we pass a drive-up ice cream joint.

There's a bunch of kids outside. "They're lucky they've got that," I say. "Their parents are lucky. But what's after? Where do they go?"

I'm thinking about the opioid statistics Joe Defino shared with me—the sense of hopelessness among too many young people.

When I was a kid, the Los Angeles public school system offered voluntary religious instruction. One day a week, whatever neighborhood you came from, you could leave class early for whatever church or temple your family went to. Didn't matter if you came from South Central or the suburbs, everybody got the same opportunity.

That's not as common as it used to be. School districts are worried about liabilities. And back then, about 90 percent of people identified as members of a religion. Now it's fewer than 60 percent.

I don't believe in forcing faith on anyone. But it can fill a gap in communities. It can make young people feel grounded—give them a sense of belonging and connection to something beyond themselves. It's an alternative to going home and sitting alone, playing video games, or scrolling online chat boards.

In the SUV's front passenger seat, Johnny knows what's on my mind just from hearing me think aloud. He nods and pokes me with his elbow.

"Hey, bro, don't underestimate the power of ice cream," he says, and points out the window.

Spoken like a true Bronx boy trying to lighten up his buddy.

I look over at him. "That so?"

"Absolutely." He smiles. "The menu says they even have orange creamsicle. We ought to check it out."

That gets me smilng too.

"Maybe we should," I say, and pull into the ice cream joint's lot.

A little after eight the next morning, John pings me with a text:

> Team Strawberry
> Today we will be visiting the Kelders at RYAN House at 11 AM.
> We should leave the hotel by 10:55.

Tonight we need to be at Cantine Field by 5 PM.

We will leave the hotel at 4:45.

We will be following someone to the complex.

I'm still dripping from the shower when John calls about forty minutes later.

"Morning," I say.

"Did you get my message?"

"I did! Eleven o'clock. RYAN House."

"We should meet in the lobby about ten minutes before. Joe Defino's coming to bring us over."

"Got it."

"That's ten fifty."

"Right."

"It's five minutes away. Shouldn't be more. But we want to be on time. These are great people—they can't wait to show us the place."

"I got you, brother."

John pauses. "They're predicting thunderstorms later this afternoon. I hope it doesn't rain out the tournament."

I turn to the window. The sky's hazy, but it doesn't look too threatening yet.

"Guess we'll see."

"If it rains, maybe we can set up a tent."

"I'm not worried," I reassure him. "If it's God's will, the event happens. He'll give us what we need to make it happen."

That gives John a boost.

"Absolutely," he says. "Meanwhile, you feel like some breakfast?"

I tell him I'll skip it. My stomach's still working off last night's meal—and that orange creamsicle soft serve.

You might get the impression that John's a nuisance, and I can confirm he is. But he's the kind of nuisance I wouldn't want to be without. When you crisscross the country—and time zones—as much as I do, it's easy to lose track of where you're supposed to be, when you need to be there, and who's going to be your point of contact. I've been known to forget which airport I'm landing in, and even which hotel I'm supposed to be checking into that day.

I like to prepare, but stay loose and receptive to people. John allows me that luxury. He makes sure I get where I'm going on time and manages everything that distracts from the purpose of my visit. His attention to planning and detail lets me focus on what really matters.

Beyond that, John's a prayer machine. When he prays, he does it from the deepest part of his being, with a soulfulness everyone around him can feel. His generosity knows no bounds—he'd give the shirt off his back to someone in need, and then hand over the rest of his clothes if it came to that.

I guess you could say he's my spiritual brother in arms.

By ten forty-five, we're in the hotel lobby with my son when Joe Defino walks in, right on time. Vince and Carole are waiting outside RYAN House when we pull up.

The building's exactly what you'd expect an old Knights of Columbus hall to look like in a small town like Saugerties—big and grand, with white siding, tall windows, and four columns under a triangle-shaped roof over the front steps.

There are flower beds on either side of the stairs. Carole points to some green shoots coming up through the dry brown stems left over from winter.

"The mums are starting to come back," she says. "They say not to pull the dead stuff too soon—it helps the roots grow stronger." She smiles and shrugs. "Ugly now. But it's getting there."

That's how she and Vince talk about the house too. Every part of it is being fixed up—one room at a time—with help from volunteers, donations, and their own hands-on work.

They'll tell you their son, Ryan, was a good student growing up. Funny, outgoing. His sister, Randi, says he had a way of making people smile. Things changed after he left for college and was prescribed Xanax for anxiety—just one pill a day. But one turned into more. Too many more. Then he got other pills after an injury. After that, people started noticing something was off.

By the time his family found out he was using heroin, he was already deep into it. He spent the rest of his short life trying to get clean, but the addiction never let go.

Vince and Carole always call addiction "progressive and deadly." Again, like any disease. And also like any disease, it's easier to fight if you catch it early.

Walking through RYAN House, it's easy to see they're trying to turn something painful into something good. The house is being rebuilt piece by piece, the way they hope people can rebuild their lives.

Addiction tears people apart. This place is meant to bring them back together.

Ryan was in and out of rehab the last two years of his life. He spent ten months in a state treatment center, got clean, and finished the program. In August 2015, Social Services placed him in a run-down apartment in a struggling village. Two weeks later, Vince found him on the kitchen floor.

He had overdosed.

"You sit in your apartment in your head with mental illness," Vince says, trying to describe how lonely and dark those final weeks must have felt.

Vince has been in recovery himself for almost thirty years and hasn't touched drugs or alcohol in all that time. What kept him going after Ryan died were the same Twelve-Step principles that helped him get clean. Instead of getting bitter or shutting down, Vince decided to help others. He and Carole realized Ryan's story might be able to save someone else. So they got to work.

There's light everywhere in RYAN House. The sun comes through the big windows and hits a small memorial to Ryan near the entrance. Upstairs, Vince and Carole are dividing rooms into dorms for young men moving from rehab back into the world. You can still smell fresh paint and the floors shine.

The place is all clean and bright, and that's no accident. Vince knows many recovery programs are underfunded and run on almost nothing, so they meet in cramped storefronts or church basements, packing up folding chairs after every session. People struggling with addiction already feel like they don't belong, and those dim, makeshift spaces only make depression worse. It's about mental health.

RYAN House's recovery program is based on the Alcoholics Anonymous and Narcotics Anonymous model that worked for Vince, and both organizations hold regular meetings in the clubhouse. But the Kelders also host game day gatherings and movie nights, with an outdoor area that includes a barbecue and brick pizza oven.

Sometimes the best support comes from people going through the same things you are. They understand challenges others can't—even when you aren't able to explain them.

I can see why that fits me. As a former ballplayer, I've always thought of the clubhouse as a place of mutual support. It's where I knew I was with people who understood me—and who I understood—because we were all going through the same things. Physically, mentally, and emotionally.

I was drafted as an eighteen-year-old, straight out of high school. There was never a time in my career when an adult's advice meant more—or when a teammate who understood my struggles, could give me advice, and have my back had a greater impact.

At some point during my tour, I start remembering my earliest years in the game, when I felt so much like an outsider I almost quit and went home to Crenshaw. That's probably because my mind's been on what I want to say to the young players at that afternoon's tournament. I feel a deep responsibility to reach those kids.

I leave RYAN House inspired by its example of community making a difference. I'm also still thinking about those tough early seasons in the minors—especially my second, in Lynchburg, Virginia.

We don't always realize the moment we gain a deeper understanding of ourselves and our place in the world until long after it happens. What I want to do at the ballfield later is like what those men did for me.

They chose to be mentors. It's another step in carrying the torch and knowing when to pass it on.

"Hope it doesn't rain," John says from the passenger seat. "It's getting cloudy."

"Everything will work out."

"Absolutely," John says. I feel like I've heard that before. "Meanwhile, I'm starving. We oughtta have lunch."

"Sure, buddy. Anywhere in particular?"

"There's a tavern next to the hotel. The barbecued short ribs are unbelievable."

I give him a look.

"What is it?"

"We ate with everyone at the restaurant last night. Then went for ice cream."

"So?"

"So, when did you find time for ribs?"

He shrugs and does that thing with both hands. *Mangia, mangia.* "I'm Italian. I know good food. Trust me."

I'm not sure that really answers my question. But I leave it right there and find a spot to pull in.

I'm in my room ahead of my talk with the teenaged baseball players, stretched out on the bed, my Bible on the nightstand. There's still a little while before I need to leave for Cantine Field, so I do some reading, some thinking, and some resting up.

That's when Lynchburg comes back to me again. It was 1981, and I was with the Mets' Class-A minor league affiliate there. The year before, I'd gotten my feet wet as a rookie with the Mets' Appalachian League team in Kingsport, Tennessee, ten or fifteen miles from Virginia's southern border. My first manager, Chuck Hiller, was a great guy—I'd describe him as loose and easy—and he really helped with my transition from high school and Crenshaw.

Tennessee had a short season of forty games or so, and my goals there were pretty much the same as at Crenshaw: get better, enjoy the experience. One of my closest buddies on the team, a catcher named Lloyd McClendon, was three years older than me. He took the college route to baseball, attending Valparaiso University, not far from where he grew up in Gary, Indiana—which explained our age difference. Back then, Gary's population was 70 percent working-class Black, and Valparaiso was a mostly white school in a suburban area that wasn't always welcoming to people of color. So, as a college player, Big Mac had already dealt with situations I hadn't.

Being away from Los Angeles for the first time, away from my family, I felt like an outsider. There was definitely some culture shock. I'd show up at Coach Hiller's office, just wanting to talk, and he'd always ask me to come in and sit down. At night after games I would call my mom collect, and tell her how lost I felt.

She'd say to give things a chance: "You made a decision to play baseball, and need to figure it out." I remember once she told me she almost fainted dead away after getting the phone bill. In those days, long-distance rates were sky high, and she said that the money I sent home from my signing bonus with the Mets was all going to Pacific Bell.

I couldn't escape the reality that the South was different from what I was used to. At Crenshaw, I'd mostly played with Black teammates, in front of Black crowds. Now there were no Black people at all in the stands. The home fans were always kind—I think they were curious about this kid who was supposed to be the second coming of Ted Williams—though

I'd hear some insults rumbling from the crowd on the road. That was new to me. In LA, we sometimes competed against white schools, but I don't remember hearing that kind of racial slur.

I was in Kingsport for maybe five or six weeks. It went by fast. I didn't exactly get the scoreboard smoking, but I held my own, and the Mets organization was optimistic I'd improve the next year.

The discrimination I experienced in Lynchburg was pretty raw. I'm not too sure why the racial divide felt wider—or more open—than in Tennessee. I do know it was an area where integration still met resistance, with prejudice built deep in the culture. The city was going through tough economic times. Most of its main industries had moved out, downtown shops were dark, and people were bitter. Maybe those hardships made things worse. I can only guess.

But understanding the reasons back then wouldn't have made things easier. I just wanted to play baseball. I didn't expect to be called derogatory names by my home fans. I never imagined that. The longer it went on, the more I struggled on the field—and the worse it got. I'd hear the yapping with every out at the plate:

"Sit down, boy! Go back where you came from!"

"You ain't no Ted Williams! Not even close!"

"Who do you think you are, nigger?"

Who? I was nineteen, trying to develop into a Major League ballplayer and figure things out. I was busy working on my game. I wasn't really thinking about who I was.

So, I withdrew. I hardly went out after we played. I truly feared what might happen to me in a place like that. I used to think the people shouting from the stands would jump me and hang me from a tree. My spirit sank, my hopes drained, and I didn't know where to turn.

It didn't help that Big Mac wasn't with the team. We were supposed to be roommates that year, but the Mets had invited him to spring training, where he broke his wrist. So he was back in Florida to start the season. Lloyd was like an older brother, and without him, I felt isolated.

I kept thinking, *Man, this isn't for me. I don't want to listen to all this craziness. I'm still young. I can go back to school, play some basketball. Pick up baseball again if I really want to.*

At that age, I never stopped to think about Hank Aaron, Willie Mays, and Jackie Robinson—great players of color who went through hell at the big-league level, on the national stage. If I'd understood what they endured to be successful—if I had even the slightest *clue*—I might've been inspired to stick it out instead of falling into bad habits. But I was young. I wasn't thinking about everything that happened to them, the ground they broke for future generations.

I started sleeping in, smoking weed, and showing up late to the ballpark.

My roommate during that time was a pitching prospect who never made the majors, and he was the only friend I had in town. Though he was a white kid from Maryland, he saw and heard the taunts being hurled at me—and more. Back then, when a white player hit a home run, the fans would pass around a hat and give him a $50 bonus. Black player? No hat.

I could tell it really disgusted him.

"You don't need all this," he'd tell me. "You don't need people calling you names."

He meant well. He loved me and thought he was looking out for me. But we were heading down a road that was bad for both of us.

I was incredibly fortunate to have Gene "Geno" Dusan as the team's manager. Once, I went AWOL for a couple of days—just stayed in the apartment and smoked marijuana. Though Gene was concerned about my unexplained absence, he protected me and kept quiet about it. If he'd informed the Mets brass, they might've booted me off the team. As their top prospect, I got a longer leash than most, but it wasn't endless.

Geno picked up on what was going on inside me, and saw I was close to the edge. I was still carrying all the unresolved anger from my childhood, and there were times I wanted to jump into the stands and end the verbal abuse with my Louisville Slugger.

Thankfully Geno saw it and stepped in. He'd invite me to his home, ask me to babysit his kids, and always wait for the right moment to explain those people were ignorant and products of an environment that reinforced that ignorance. He said they weren't using their heads, but probably drinking too much, and just going along with what they thought was expected. I found it hard to understand at the time, but when he advised me not to take it personally and to concentrate on my game, I tried my best to ignore them.

About a third of the way through our season, we got some good news from Florida. Big Mac was healthy enough for him to rejoin the club and Geno didn't waste any time bringing him up. He'd just gotten married to his college sweetheart, and was going to rent his own apartment.

But Gene had other plans.

One day right after Lloyd got back, I'd smoked some weed and was in the locker room high as a kite. He just stood at his locker, gave me a long look, and shook his head.

"What is *wrong* with you?" he asked.

That was a loaded question. I didn't know where to start, or how to put it all into words. So I kind of stumbled. "Man, this place . . . it's crazy here."

He cut me off. "You're moving out of your room," he said. "And you're moving in with me."

There was nothing to think about. We were supposed to be roommates before he got hurt. I'd missed him and couldn't have felt any lonelier. I packed my stuff as soon as I got home from the park.

What I didn't know was that Geno had already talked to him about everything that was going on with me. He told him he had to take care of me, and that I wouldn't make it if he didn't. Gene Dusan knew we'd wind up rooming together before I did, because he was behind it. It was all his idea.

Things changed after that. I finally had my rock-solid big brother back, and I remember him sitting me down for a talk. I opened up to

My mother, Ruby. The reason
I'm living another life today.

Mom and me being introduced
to New York City.

Mom's support at my first marriage.

Visiting Death Row at Angola Prison was one of the most powerful and humbling experiences of my life.

Preaching the Word at a prison and bringing lost souls to salvation.

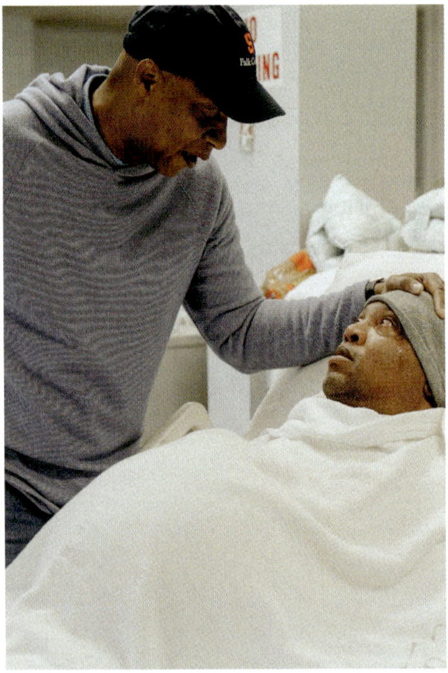

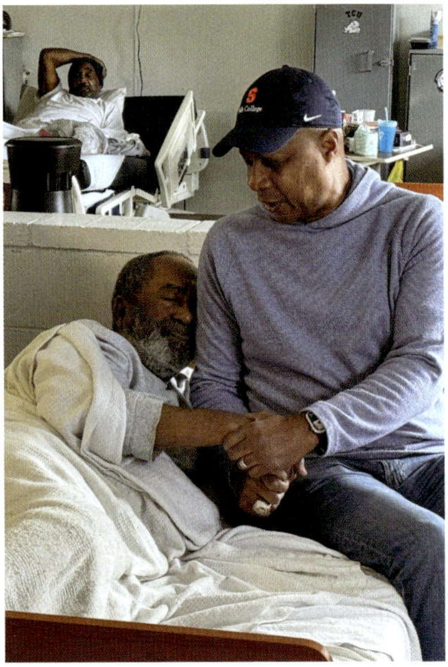

The hospice at Angola Prison, where inmates serving life sentences will spend their final days. This was a wonderful opportunity for me to extend God's grace and mercy over their lives.

him, and told him I was thinking of going home to California, but he wouldn't hear it.

"Hang in there. Keep your head on right," he told me. "I know things can be tough, but you have to deal with it."

Big Mac would say I needed to "regulate" my body. He made sure I'd get up early, go to movies or the mall. He didn't want me just lying around the apartment, smoking pot, grabbing a bite, and then heading over to the park for the game. He believed in getting himself physically and mentally ready to play, and he made me go along with the routine. We'd take extra batting practice together almost every day.

Without Geno and Lloyd McClendon, I would have never made it. They gave me something different, taught me about more than being a baseball player. They made me realize not everything was going to be fair, but that it didn't mean you should shut yourself in a box and seal its lid up tight.

In my Saugerties hotel room half a lifetime later, the kindness I was shown by those two men—one white, one Black—fills my heart like it was yesterday. I think of what a gift it was to play baseball with such a supportive manager and teammate. And I think of the blessing—yes, blessing—it was to go through those hard times in Lynchburg.

I'm a strong believer that God puts storms in all our lives so we can learn from them and grow into who we're meant to become. A lot of times people look at the beginning of a journey to measure its value. But God doesn't look at the beginning. God looks at the destination, the last part of the journey.

You're going to go through it, but He's going to get it out of you. If He gives you success all at once, when you start out, you wouldn't value it the same way you do when it comes at the end.

As I think about this, and the lessons I want to share with the high school players I'm about to speak to, I know exactly what I want to say to them.

It didn't rain.

The Hope Rocks Hardball Invitational at Cantine Field brings together eight of the best high school teams from nearby areas that usually meet in state tournaments. For some, it's a bus ride of an hour or more—a real commitment for the coaches. They've got games all week, jobs, and give up time with family to make it happen. But it all comes down to community.

At the event, speakers talk throughout the day. A multiple suicide attempt survivor talks about battling self-destructive thoughts and fighting suicide through selflessness and kindness. Another covers how teenagers can manage depression and anxiety. A third talks about nutrition for a healthy brain.

Joe Defino put this all together: counselors, groups, and families under one big tent. It's about rebuilding lives and making help easier to get when someone's in crisis.

As I walk onto the field, both teams pack the bleachers, all in uniform. I've brought my Bible—I always do—but I know these kids come from every faith, or none at all, and my message is for everyone. I can tell they want to hear me, but they're ready to get at it. They came to play baseball, and I won't keep them from it long.

I start by pointing out something they probably know, even if they don't realize it yet: Being athletes and part of a team is something special. Everybody wants to feel connected with a circle of friends, and in baseball, you have that.

"In my day, we didn't have cell phones or the internet," I say. "When we were on the road, we only had each other. And it got to be the same for life situations. It wasn't that we were smart. We thought we were knuckleheads. But young people can be wiser than anyone gives them credit for—including themselves. We knew we were going down that road together. And if we were going to reach our goals, we had to be open about our struggles. We couldn't judge each other. Each of us had to give part of ourselves to one another."

I pause and look at their young faces. I see a little of myself in all of them. Then I think of Gene Dusan, Big Mac, the coaches and teammates who helped me from high school through the majors. And I hope these kids will see me as that kind of guy—someone who showed up and kept it honest.

"Everything I just talked about—you can do it, if things aren't blocking you. And by that I mean the things that make you feel judged, that build walls. The same internet that connects you can also make you feel lonely and isolated."

I let my eyes move from one boy to the next. "How many of you use social media?"

They all raise their hands.

"So everybody wants that 'like,' huh?" I say. It gets a laugh. "And when you don't see enough of them—huge problem, right?"

Their laughter spreads through the bleachers. I'm glad. It means they're listening, and that's the first step. There's never a guarantee. I've sat at roundtables with teens facing addiction. It's hard for them to open up.

Usually, it starts the same way: I'll ask, "Tell me about your family life."

"Pretty good. My parents are never around."

Then I ask, "What happens?"

"You just feel lonely."

"What do you do?"

They'll all shrug. "I've learned to connect with people on these," they say, holding up their phones. "I connect with people on the internet."

When I ask what that means, they don't hesitate. "You can always find a party where everybody's getting high. And if you don't feel like you fit in, there's another place to go. There's always somewhere to be."

That's what they tell me, again and again. I've gone from one place to another and heard the same stories. Different faces, different parts of the country, same story: Lonely at home. Lonely in the community you grew up in. First you're isolated. Then you find a group to get high with. You're most comfortable being around each other when you're all high.

And it's not always kids without resources. These can be kids in the suburbs, going to good schools. They've got what they need. Some are driving their own cars. But nobody's really paying attention, and that's how drugs take over.

What I want the high school players to know is you can make a bunch of bad decisions and maybe find your way back. But it only takes one—*one*—and your life could be cut short. At my lowest point, I put a needle in my arm to shoot heroin. I knew I'd crossed a line. I was coming into that place of being a full junkie, and I had to make a change.

That was a terrible mistake, and thank the Lord I survived it. But with fentanyl and opioids and potent drugs like that, there's no room for mistakes. Fentanyl is fifty times stronger than heroin. At sixty-three, working with people in recovery, I'm seeing kids under twenty die from overdoses or suicide at the highest rate I've ever come across. And it breaks my heart because I know there's a solution.

What is it?

"Just don't start," I tell the players. "Don't pick up alcohol. Don't pick up pot or pills."

It sounds almost too easy, like a slogan. Plenty say that—without ever walking through the storm. If those kids heard it from them, they might not listen, and I'd understand. *I* didn't listen when I heard it back in the 1980s. But I'm someone who's made every mistake you can name and lived it out in public.

I've talked about this before—how, when I met Tracy, she was dragging me out of crack houses in South Florida. Fighting people to get between me and drugs. Kicking in doors. Putting herself in danger to save me when I didn't want saving. She'd say God had a plan for me. I'd snap at her, ask why she and God wouldn't just leave me there to die. And she'd yell back I wasn't that lucky.

The kids might not know all of this, and they don't need to, though I've never made a secret of it. What they do know is I'm speaking from experience, and hopefully it helps them trust me.

"And if you can't, you can trust this," I tell them, and raise the Bible. Like with my own kids, I don't push anything on them, but I can only share what's been real in my own life. "A simple book for complicated people. The book that contains the sacred Word of God. When I lost everything else, that's what stayed."

Then I step back and tell them to go have a good time out there. Before heading to their dugouts, they ask to take snapshots with me and tell this old ballplayer how much their dads loved watching me play.

A few minutes later, I'm talking to the people who've come to watch the game. I see Vince and Carole Kelder, Joe Defino, and some of the others from last night's dinner. We talk for a while as Jordan snaps a few pictures, and then John Luppo comes up to me.

"So," I say. "What do you think?"

He looks up at the sky.

"It's a beautiful night," he says.

I nod. Beautiful, ordinary, and *special* at the same time.

We stand there a minute in the breeze, and then turn and watch the kids take the field.

Chapter Ten

Home

I don't know the weight limit on a Mitsubishi hatchback, but if anyone can test it, it's Tracy on a supermarket run.

I hear her pull up behind the house and stop near the kitchen door, and I can see the back of the car is full of groceries. It's like she's delivering to an army.

My eyes still puffy from sleep, I come outside in my sweatpants and slippers. After two weeks on the road and a red-eye from LA, I got home early that morning—or late the night before, however you want to look at it. When she left, I was out cold.

"You did a little shopping."

"A little." She pops the hatch, halfway out the driver's door. "The kids might be coming over."

"Uh-huh."

Sometimes it's the kids; other times, it's the girls from the Dream Center in Troy, Missouri, where they're working through addiction, abuse, and other issues.

Trace shops like a mother, a wife, and a pastor all in one.

I grab three of the heaviest-looking bags and bring them inside, one tucked into my left side, one on my right, and one balanced up against my chest. That one's got my cookies and cereal, so I want to be careful not to crush them.

Tracy does the unpacking. On my third trip from the car, I see her dig two packages from the meat department out of a bag—chicken breast and frozen beef. I slide a couple of bags aside on the counter to make room for what I just brought in. That takes care of every last inch of space.

"Street tacos or smash burgers for lunch?" she says.

"Yeah."

"Don't push your luck."

She checks her watch. "Graduation's in an hour," she says. "I'll be back around noon."

"I should go."

"No, rest up. You'll see everyone at church tomorrow."

We unload more bags—dish soap, laundry detergent, spray cleaner. Ice cream, soda, coffee. This goes in the fridge, that up in the cabinet. Tracy says my arms are like tree trunks, so I get cabinet duty.

I like doing this with her. When she first took me to Walmart, it was a serious *trip*. Before that, I didn't even know you could buy groceries and socks together in the same store . . . at a bargain! Tracy didn't just pull me out of debt. She didn't hand me a quick fix. She went to the root of my spending, challenged my ideas about relying on material things for my happiness, showed me what it means to be sensible with finances, and encouraged me to take pride in it.

She helped me see I'd been trying to fill a space that buying stuff could never fill.

I remember once when a friend from New York came to visit. A day or two before his flight, he lost a filling and couldn't get to a dentist. You know when the edges of a cavity scrape against your tongue? After a while, your tongue starts to swell up.

It sounded like our friend had a ball of wool in his mouth when he talked, but he didn't say why at first. I guess he was a little embarrassed.

We were driving somewhere when it got so bad he could barely talk, so hc finally told us.

Trace knows all about the over-the-counter remedies you can pick up at places like CVS or Rite Aid—the kind of stuff you get when you can't quite get to a doctor or dentist.

"Darryl, pull in over there." She pointed up ahead toward the entrance to an outdoor mall. "This won't take five minutes."

Tracy scooted into the pharmacy. Four minutes later, she climbed back into the SUV, bag in hand.

"I bought temporary filling and dental wax," she said, handing it to him over the seat. "First, put in the filling. When it hardens, smooth the wax over the sharp spots with your finger."

Our friend looked at her like he'd been given the secret code for whatever.

"I never even heard of this wax," he said. "How do you know about it?"

She took a breath, and I knew why.

"When some of the residents first come in, their teeth are pretty bad," she said. "It could be drugs, or just not getting any care. I picked up the same thing last week for one of the women—she was homeless."

Tracy's good at the little things that make a big difference. Part of it comes natural for her, and part of it's guided by something bigger than herself. She worked out a Christ-based study course for the Dream Center that helps residents rebuild their lives, every day, step by step, with God.

Some of the residents didn't grow up with any structure. No one showed them how to take care of a place or themselves. Just having a schedule is new to them. So when they get to the center, it starts small. Making the bed. Taking a shower every day. Cooking breakfast. Doing laundry. For someone who's never had a stable home, it could be that sweeping a floor or showing up for chores is the first time they're responsible for anything.

But none of that sticks unless they get to the root of their addictions. That starts with discipleship—a big word that just means learning and growing in faith through Bible mentorship and serving others.

A few months ago, the women's residence wasn't even part of the Dream Center; it used to be run by another program that did great work but couldn't keep up financially. Tracy says it's a common story. A lot of ministries and recovery places struggle not because they don't care, but because they don't know how to budget.

That's where her background in business and ministry leadership makes a real difference. The Dream Center is a calling, but it has an executive board that makes decisions like any other boardroom. Tracy's on it, and with God's help, she steered them through the financial realities. Through a solid plan and prayer, they took over the residence and made sure the women there weren't left stranded. Instead, they're graduating the first part of the program. That makes it extra special.

Once the groceries are all put away, Tracy checks the time again and gets herself together. It's a short drive to Troy, but she wants to be there early. They're serving cake and soft drinks after the ceremony, and she wants to help with the setup.

"See you later." She plants one on me and then wipes off the lipstick. "I'll say hi to everyone for you."

And she's out the door.

June was a busy month.

I had a preaching engagement in New Jersey. A signing event at the unreal flagship MLB store near Rockefeller Center in Manhattan, commemorating the one-year anniversary of my number retirement. Lines stretched up and down the block from Fifth to Sixth Avenue—I was amazed and humbled by the loyalty of Mets fans. After that, I led a

Father's Day service honoring dads at a Los Angeles church. Then it was back to New York for a Long Island golf tournament raising money for families affected by autism.

I'm leaving out a few stops. Thankful as I am for every one of them, I'm glad to be home for the next ten days or so. It's only been a year since I was just getting back on my feet after the heart attack.

I grab a cold soda from the fridge and flop down on the couch, staring out the patio doors. Trace says she hasn't seen the geese for about a week; I guess that's just when they usually stop hanging around the lake. Last year they came back, nested, then left again. They've made a few miles.

The deer, on the other hand, are still out there doing their thing.

We built a screened gazebo in the yard, not too big, just enough for a picnic table and chairs. I like going out early to read the Bible and meditate while the birds chirp. Nearby, there's a barbecue pit, a swing set, and monkey bars for when family visits. Tracy put up a plaque outside the screen door, offering a blessing for the gazebo as a place of peace, contemplation, and togetherness.

This is home. I've lived in gated communities, huge multimillion-dollar houses, and none of them came close to giving me the peace I find here.

You can have everything and have nothing inside. That's how I was once. I had everything—and had nothing. You can buy another expensive car, another house, and think it's going to fill the emptiness. Maybe it does, for a moment. But it's like an adrenaline rush. It wears off.

Being an evangelist is a blessing I thank God for every day, and it's all grounded in being a husband and father to my kids. When I preach and tell people my story, I don't dress it up. I say it plain and raw: My father treated us like crap. I don't say that to put him down, or to vent. I don't mean to be disrespectful, but I want others who have suffered abuse to know I understand their feelings.

To anyone in that situation, I want to say you aren't alone. I've been in your shoes. And there's a way out. I promise, you can break the chain.

That starts with getting well. Someone in the chain has to decide to get well. I got well so my kids would never have to experience the things I did.

The home Tracy and I have made for ourselves is a testament to that.

I grab a cold soda and the remote and turn on the TV to see when the Mets and Yankees are playing. I don't get to watch much baseball anymore with all the travel, but I try to keep up when I can. I'm devoted to my calling. But I've come to know baseball wasn't separate from that—it was part of how He shaped me.

Those years still mean a lot to people. The game brings them joy. And every now and then, it opens a door—for someone who otherwise might never hear what I have to say, baseball gives me a way in. That's something I've come to really value.

New York will always have a special place in my heart. Not just for the energy, but for the feeling of winning a championship that the whole city gets behind. These days, people are dealing with a lot—money stress, politics, everything. There's pressure coming from every direction. But when a team wins in New York? That's unmatched. Indescribable. It pulls people together and gives everyone a lift.

I realize I've embraced a different kind of path, and part of what I most enjoy now is getting to share both sides of my life—baseball and faith—with Jordan.

Since his son Jaydin was born a few months ago, he's been different. We've had a lot of talks lately. Sometimes in a restaurant in whatever city we're in. Sometimes driving late at night, with nothing but *time* to talk. It's like this running conversation we keep picking back up.

One night, he asked me how I really came to believe . . . how I changed. I told him I always had faith, but it took losing everything before I let God rebuild me.

He didn't say much. But I can tell he's thinking hard about what kind of man and father *he* wants to be.

At the MLB store signing in New York, two of my closest friends showed up with their kids to surprise us, and we were all amazed by the turnout for someone who hadn't taken the field in twenty-five years. I tried to give everyone an extra minute to talk or snap a picture. It matters that we show gratitude to others.

What I want Jordan to see is that when you're honest and let God work through you, He'll meet you where you are and make things possible you didn't expect. It's a message I hope he'll pass on now that he's a father.

The channel guide says the Mets aren't playing till late afternoon. Three months into the season, Pete Alonso, the first baseman they were asking me about back at Port St. Lucie, is at 243 career home runs—ten short of breaking my franchise record. I'm sure he's going to do it this year. When he will is the only question.

I'm thinking the end of July, or maybe August. And like I told Keith and Ron on television, I'm rooting for Pete. He had his struggles and issues with the front office. But he got an opportunity to come back. I didn't come back, and I'm glad he could.

You're talking about a record that's been there a very long time, thirty-seven years, and nobody's gotten close but David Wright. And now Pete's right there knocking at the door—a homegrown player developed through the farm system just like me.

I don't want my record to stand. Once you've done it, no one can ever take it away from you, and I'm not a player anymore. I'm a man outside of baseball, and passing the torch to the next generation is what baseball's all about. It's for the young guys.

But for now, Pete's next one has to wait. Since the Mets aren't on yet, I click over to the Yankees. There's still some time before the game, and I reach for the blanket Tracy left folded at the end of the couch. She was right. I'm really feeling my cross-country preaching marathon (it's the red-eyes and four-hour layovers that get me), so I cover myself and settle in.

The blanket's soft and fluffy, and I pull it up to my chin before the game starts.

Ten minutes later, I'm dead to the world.

The sound of the back door opening and closing wakes me. On the TV, the Yankees are down 1–0 to the Athletics, top of the fourth. I sit straight and turn to see Tracy come in.

"How'd the graduation go?"

"Couldn't have gone better," she says. "That group was so proud. I love seeing them like that."

"When you think about how they were before," I say, "it's a pretty amazing thing."

I yawn and stretch. Trace puts down her purse.

"They're having an intake at the men's residence Monday," she says. "Also, Emil's giving a tour. I'd love for you to be there."

Emil Moore's the pastor who leads the Dream Center. He's on the executive board with Tracy.

"You got it."

I reach way up and stretch again. Trace opens the fridge and looks at me over her shoulder.

"So?" she asks. "What did you decide?"

"Smash burgers," I say. "But can we have tacos tomorrow?"

Later in the game, with the Yankees still getting shut out, I flip over to the Mets on SNY. They're playing Pittsburgh on the road.

I'm carrying our plates to the sink when I hear Gary Cohen say something that stops me cold. Dave Parker has passed. The Pirates made the announcement before the start of the game.

I stand there a second, just listening. They roll through his career—his MVP year, the cannon arm, the batting titles. They mention how he was finally going to be inducted into the Hall of Fame by one of the special committees. The honor came. Just too late.

"The Cobra," I say. "Man."

We shook hands a few times at baseball events, but I didn't know him personally—his best years were before my playing days. Growing up in LA before cable and streaming, I only followed the Dodgers on local TV. Then one time I watched them play the Pirates and saw Parker in right. Big, strong, a 6'5" lefthander. He could run, throw, and hit with power.

I said to myself, *I want to be like that.*

He could beat you five different ways, and made it look easy.

And he should've been in the Hall way before now.

I always look forward to Sunday services with Tracy when I'm not on the road.

The church we go to in Troy isn't particular about what you wear. Some people dress up, some come in jeans and a tee. Their philosophy is that God looks at your heart, not your clothes, and I agree with that. We keep it casual, though for Trace that still means a snazzy blazer. I stick to chinos and a golf shirt, though shopping for chinos long enough for a 6'6" beanstalk is its own kind of prayer.

When we chose Journey Church, it was all about finding somewhere to worship and serve in our community. We didn't want attention. We wanted to stay out of the spotlight and be ourselves. And we found just what we were looking for, a place that was welcoming and cared for its neighbors quietly and in line with God's principles.

I love the drive. The road goes straight through Missouri farming country, and we pass lots of cornfields, some barns and silos for storing grain, and stretches of trees. There are small towns or houses with gas stations and diners. Otherwise, it's just the quiet, and that puts me in a peaceful state of mind.

Every now and then, I imagine what Mead Chasky would think of all this. I'm pretty sure he thinks corn starts out in a supermarket bin, like it doesn't have to grow anywhere.

We get to church during the second song. Some of the men and women from the Dream Center are already there, and I recognize most of them. Tracy knows them all and she's hugging people the second we step out of the SUV.

Well, that isn't exactly right. She's hugging some of the women through the window while we're pulling in. Then again after we get out. And again in the lobby—asking how they're doing, asking about their families and other disciples like she's known them forever.

Pastor Emil's preaching today. He's doing a Summer Movie Series, which I guess means picking a different movie each week and tying it into his message. Today it's *Remember the Titans.* He plays the who's-your-daddy clip where Denzel lays into that linebacker: "Is this your team, or is this your daddy's team?"

A few people laugh. When Emil asks how many people haven't seen the movie, maybe three raise their hands. He's got their attention.

He says, "These dudes all had their own ideas about how things were gonna go. But if they wanted that title, they had to get out of their own way." Then he asks, "How many times have you told God what you want, and exactly when you want it? But that's not how it works. You have to get out of your own way and trust His plan."

It's not how I usually preach, and I like that. We bring our own styles, take different paths to the same place. There's nothing tired about the way Emil does it. He preaches without being preachy. People can relate to what he's saying, take it home with them, and apply it to their everyday lives. The Bible's *meant* to be lived, not just read and explained in the same words we've heard a thousand times. We need to put it into practice.

When it's time to pray, Tracy stands and moves to the front like she always does, laying on hands, picking up on who needs support. Our worship team is amazing onstage. The drummer's in one of those sound booths like a rock star, slamming it with his sticks and bass pedal. It's really unbelievable—you get goosebumps and tremble inside. It's an energy of its own, magical and real.

When the service wraps up, Tracy and I congratulate Emil on doing a great job and make plans to meet up with him the next day at the Dream Center. Trace gives out more hugs and listens to more people confide in her, and then we head out to the SUV.

I kept my phone notifications off during the service, so I don't get the big news from Jordan until we're back home. When I finally see it, I do a double take.

"Whoa," I say.

"What?" Trace asks.

"Wow," I say, speechless, holding out the phone to her.

Trace raises an eyebrow and smiles, reading the text twice. It's from Jordan—five or six photos. He's waist-deep in a baptismal pool, his eyes closed, water dripping from his face. The pastor's got a hand on his back and another on his chest.

My grandson Jaydin's still crawling, but his daddy just stood up.

"He went and did it," I say. "Got baptized."

I couldn't have imagined a better surprise. Jordan doesn't talk much about what's on his mind. He's quiet and soft-spoken, but there's a lot under the surface. Still waters run deep.

I feel such pride in that moment. I wasn't around for many of the crucial parts of his life—his early childhood, his teenage years. I tried to be the best dad I could, but he grew up mostly with his mom—my first wife, Charisse—in California during the dark days I was battling drug and alcohol addiction. And he knew about those times. He saw me go through them from far away. It was all public.

By the time Jordan started playing basketball for Mercer University around 2015, I was clean and sober twelve years, a born-again Christian, liberated by the power of God. I was ready to be a true father, if he could accept it. I'm grateful he did.

At first, I guess we bonded around being athletes. But I felt I needed to take an active role in his future. I wanted Mercer's coaching staff to make sure he did everything he needed to do to develop. I told them to keep it on his butt.

So we saw traveling together as a win-win. A chance for us to build a better relationship while getting his life on track. You bet I also wanted him to grow his relationship with God. But if that happened, I never wanted him doing it for me. I wanted it to be his personal decision. By being with me every day and seeing the power of my purpose, he'd get a chance to see the joy and healing it brings people. I wanted to set an example.

Trace hands me the phone.

"How's that feel?"

I take the phone and just sit with it a second. There's so much. Grace, pride, healing . . . and maybe the beginning of something, not just for Jordan, but for me. Something new.

How's that feel?

I try to put it all into an answer and can't. It isn't that I don't know. I think I do. I just don't know how to say it right. Not yet.

But I've got faith the words will come.

You turn off for the Dream Center, and right before it, there's a burned-out house. Emil told me it used to be a meth lab. The place just sits there on a quiet road, caved in on itself, charred and black from fire. You can still see the chimney poking up from the mostly collapsed roof. Emil says it's a picture of what the enemy does . . . and what's up the road is what God can rebuild.

Troy, and all of Lincoln County, Missouri, is flooded with meth and fentanyl. It's the same story as Saugerties. The car plant helps. It brings more jobs, and I'm glad for that. Troy's a middle-class town, and the poverty rate's just under the state average. But the meth trade has brought up violent crime, and for young people not working at the auto plant, there aren't many career prospects. A lot of them look for work in nearby cities or move away to find better opportunities.

I don't think the problem's just about jobs or crime. What's missing for a lot of young people—here and in plenty of other places—is a connection to their spiritual selves. That's what helps you hold steady when times get tough. Without it, finding real direction can be hard, no matter where you are.

It's Monday, around ten in the morning, and Tracy and I are meeting Pastor Emil at the men's residence. When it comes into view through the trees, it looks more like a lodge than what you'd ordinarily picture as a recovery center, with wood siding and wide windows. There are walking paths and nature all around. Out back on the deck, a few benches—places to sit and talk, or be by yourself.

The Dream Center isn't a clinic, and it's not supposed to look like one. I mentioned before, we call it a discipleship program. That means living like Christ, and learning to live in the world through service to others.

Disciple and discipline sound alike for a reason. You can't be one without the other.

Being a disciple means Bible study. It also means learning to cook, make a bed, wash dishes, and clean floors. Discipline, responsibility, and purpose show up in being trained to follow God, and also in the everyday work.

Most of the disciples come straight from jail or detox. Some got dropped off by family who convinced them to give it a try—if they're lucky enough to have family. No matter how they got here, this is where they start fresh. This is where the healing begins.

The program runs six to nine months, but healing and growing take a full-life commitment. There are big hills to climb. The time after detox is rough, and the enemy's ready to move in with temptation, shame, depression, and despair, to cloud people with darkness when they're at their weakest.

I once heard Emil tell a story in church. A zebra's out in the field. It's all alone, and a hungry lion sees its stripes sticking out against the grass.

"Easy to spot, right?" Emil said. Then he turned to a young man in the congregation and asked him to stand. He was tall and had on the Dream Center polo shirt all disciples wear on Sundays.

Emil cracked a joke about trying to get a jump shot over him on the basketball court, just to keep things loose. Then he asked the young men around him to stand too. There was a group—eight, nine, maybe ten. They wore the same blue-and-white Dream Center shirt. That shirt's required when you're in the program. Emil tells me every disciple wears it like a badge of honor. It's part of the commitment.

Now the guys in the group stood shoulder to shoulder in their blue-and-white shirts. The first young man was still a head above the others. But with all of them together like that in those shirts, he wasn't as easy to pick out as prey. He had brothers standing beside him, shielding him, covering him on all sides. He wasn't alone and exposed anymore.

"You see what happens when the herd closes ranks?" Emil said. "The lion moves off hoping to find an easier target."

That's what it comes down to. Brotherhood and sisterhood protect us when the enemy's circling.

Emil had a head start at being a pastor. His father was a pastor, too, so he grew up around church. But before he felt God's call, he worked in corporate sales. He was good at it and handled some of the biggest accounts in the country. It makes him a natural for showcasing the center to visitors—police, potential business donors, anyone who might want to help.

Tracy and I go along for part of this morning's tour, but Emil's in charge. He guides our visitor through the center, showing the rooms where disciples gather for morning Psalms and evening prayers. He takes him to the spaces for those meetings, where they come together to check in and support each other.

Then he brings us to the common rooms where they hang out and eat their meals. After that, we stop at quiet corners stocked with Bibles for people in recovery. That's where disciples go when they want to be alone, read, and reflect.

The intake's in about an hour, over at the women's residence, so we all head out together—me, Emil, Tracy, and our visitor.

The building used to be a rectory and now doubles as the center's main office. It's bigger than the men's and sits in a busier part of town, letting the community know the Dream Center is part of it, that they're connected, not separate.

Inside, the first thing you notice is the writing on the side of the reception counter. It's done with pens and markers, in different handwritings, and it stretches across the surface in all directions.

"Clean & Sober for 1 year! December 23, 2022 – Kathy" is scrawled in red, bold and proud near the top.

Someone else wrote, "Graduated the program 9/21/24! Got my GED! Jesus saved me, healed my heart, & delivered me completely from drug addiction." Then they added Jeremiah 29:11, and underlined "hope and a future."

Another says, "Reconnected with my parents for the first time in years! – Alicia."

"My sister gave her life to Christ – 10/9/24. Thank you, Jesus," is signed in black ink, the handwriting small but steady.

There are more, and they're never cleaned off or covered up. They're not graffiti, and they're not for decoration. They're testimonies. Emil says this is one place where you don't hide what God's done. You write it down and leave it where others can see.

In one of the front rooms, there's a silhouette on the wall—just the shape of a woman holding a long sword out at her side. No face. T-shirt and leggings, like she's geared up for something. The background's white, and under her feet it says: *Psalm 144:1–2.* That's the warrior's psalm. David wrote it when he needed God to show up, and it isn't just about physical battle—it's about spiritual readiness too. God trains your hands for battle, but you don't have to fight it alone. He's your rock and your shield.

For women coming out of trauma, addiction, or brokenness, that image—a woman warrior with no name, no face, standing on that psalm like it's her bedrock—doesn't speak of aggression. It speaks of strength. Of being equipped. Of not being alone anymore.

She could be any woman. But she's ready.

The space itself is open and clean, made to feel like home. Soft colors, curtains, flowers. Scripture on the walls. There's a cross on one wall, in the common room where they gather for study. For the women here, it's a reminder that someone already carried the weight for them. Jesus gave His life so their pain and past didn't have to define them. When He said, "It is finished," He meant the price was paid—and a new life could begin.

Emil points out the dining areas, where they meet for classes, where the staff checks them in. He knows what to show visitors. The tours help people see what they're building.

But the real work happens in moments you almost never see coming. The explosion of honesty, the breaking open. The healing that starts with just one person telling the truth.

What I wish people could feel is that moment a soul opens up. When somebody finally lets go of the thing they've been holding in.

That happens today at the intake. It's a total surprise, and it blows all of us away.

People recognize me. That's just a fact of life. Every public figure has to decide what to do with that recognition, and I've chosen to use it as a platform to make a difference. Or maybe it's more true to say God chose it for me.

Sometimes that means posing for a photo, signing a ball, or shaking someone's hand while I'm stopping at a newsstand or ordering coffee at a Starbucks in New York. Other times, it's a chance to tell someone in need of a little hope I've been where they are. That there's a way forward.

The intake at the Dream Center is a serious step for the men coming in, and could be their last chance to turn their lives around. When we show up, they're watching an orientation video in a small room off the lobby, a conference space with a screen and rows of chairs.

Emil, Tracy, and I step in toward the end. Most of the guys don't notice us at first, but when the lights come up, a few heads turn in my direction. A couple of them nudge each other. One says, "I never met a famous person before."

I shake his hand, give him a smile, and squeeze his shoulder, no speeches. I just want them to know I'm glad they're here.

The group's small—seven or eight men. But that's average for an intake, and based on open beds. Most of them are covered in tattoos, from their arms up to their necks. A few have that hardened look you get from jail time, street life, and years of addiction. One of them looks like he stepped right off a Harley—shaved head, biker beard, muscles, inked all over. Another guy's very thin and stays to the back, almost like he's trying to hide behind the rest. Tracy tells me later that he was sick, homeless, and barefoot when he came in for the first interview. The center had to get him medical treatment, and buy him clean clothes and a pair of shoes.

For all that, they're here. They walked through the door. Took that step. No one forced it on them. But you can tell they're still suspicious and doubtful. It's all over their faces. They don't trust themselves, so how can they trust anybody else? But the hope's there, mixed in with the uncertainty.

Emil asks everyone into the lobby, where he gives them a few words before they all grab some lunch. Half a dozen pizza boxes are waiting for them.

"We're going to expect a lot out of you," he says, "but we want you to expect a lot out of yourselves. And we're going to be here to help all the way."

Emil doesn't dress it up. He tells them it's going to be hard, and he means it. Probably they know it too. In some ways, what's ahead is every bit as hard as what they're walking away from.

The Dream Center isn't a rehab or a shelter. People often get confused about the difference. The men and women in a recovery program have already gone through detox. This is the next stage, where they literally recover their lives with Christ at the center. It's for dealing with depression, hopelessness, and anything else that's got control of them and led to their addiction.

The center takes care of housing, food, rides, and the basics like toiletries. Its staff keeps watch to make sure no one slips up, especially the ones just getting started who are on probation or court orders.

Tracy speaks after Emil. She lets them know she was once in a place where she lost her kids, so they realize how far down into emptiness she'd gone, and that she's faced the same self-destructiveness, shame, and guilt they're living with. Everyone here understands what it's like to be in that place, and won't quit on them as long as they don't quit on themselves.

I'm off to the side, listening and being quiet. This part belongs to Tracy and Emil, and I didn't plan to say anything. But Emil turns and asks.

I nod and step forward, thinking about what I can add.

"I just want to say . . . some of you recognized me as a baseball player, and that's because I had a lot of success," I tell them. "On the outside, I had everything. But inside, I was broken. I was a drug addict and an alcoholic. I went to jail for a year. I was a mess and it almost killed me. Whatever you're going through, I've been there. So when you see me standing here, don't think I'm any different from you. I'm only alive because I let God carry me through. And if I could make it, you can."

That's it, the most important thing I can leave them with. We don't want their ears ringing with speeches.

The intakes clap for us, and that's okay, but we all clap louder for them. They're the ones who've decided to change, and that takes courage. We want them to know we get it.

Emil's about to tell them the pizza's waiting when one of the guys—the one who looks like he rode in on a bike—raises his hand.

"Okay if I say something?"

He's the last person you'd expect to sound shy. But he does. Even when he raises his hand, he kind of hesitates, like he isn't too sure about it.

"Of course," Emil says.

The man steps forward and looks right at us.

"I want to thank you," he says. "I been out there a long time. I lost everybody. I don't have no friends. No family. Nobody to help me. Nobody that cares . . ."

He chokes up. None of us let out a sound. Tracy, Emil . . . we've all got tears in our eyes.

"So, just thank you again for giving me this chance," he finishes.

This time it's Emil who starts the clapping. His cheeks are wet.

There's a cafeteria-style table at the far end of the lobby, and some of the disciples who've been with the program awhile carry the pizza over to it. They sit and eat with the new guys, and I see them talking to them, putting their arms around their shoulders, inviting them in. I think about Emil's zebra sermon at the church. *Brotherhood and sisterhood protect us when the enemy's circling.*

It hits me that Emil used to work in corporate America. I was one of the top athletes in the world. Tracy never dreamed she'd be a pastor, a teacher, a leader of a ministry. And these men—you don't know where they come from, or what they've been through. But somehow, by God's hand, we're all here, in this room, at this moment.

To me, that's a miracle.

It's a world of miracles, if you really look at it—right in front of us, all around us. We just need to open our eyes to see them, open our hearts to welcome them in, and open our hands to share that gift with others.

That's what the power of purpose can do.

And it's Jesus Christ who gives purpose its power.

On our way home, I keep thinking about the men at the intake, especially the one who spoke up. No friends, no family, nobody to love or support him. He was thanking the people at the center, and they deserve it.

But if he sticks with the program, he'll learn to give himself credit for showing up and taking the steps to change his life—and to give God credit above all for extending the grace to open that door.

I don't know the guy's crimes or sins. I don't know what wounds he might have caused. When you're an addict, you hurt the ones you love, and who love you. But the beauty of redemption is that Jesus has already taken the punishment so you can be forgiven.

I know. When I was at my worst, I alienated many people I cared about. I wounded the people I loved most. But I would eventually be saved by grace. God extends the grace and mercy you need—you just have to receive it. And then own up to your part of the bargain by reflecting His goodness.

I turn up toward the house and drive along the edge of the lake. It's getting late in the afternoon and the light washes over us through the woods.

Tracy pats my arm. "Day in the life," she says.

"A fantastic day," I say.

She nods. "Ready for those street tacos?"

I knew she wouldn't forget. Saying I'm ready doesn't come close.

Trace makes them with chicken and beef and all the fixings that go on top. Then we get into our sweats and stretch out on the couch with a blanket over us, facing each other in our bare feet, my big clompy ones over her girly, nail-polished ones. I put on the TV. No Mets, but Yankees–Blue Jays is just wrapping up, Yankees down by one after eight.

The house is quiet. I can feel myself relaxing, but my mind's still going, back to those last few minutes at the intake.

This time I'm thinking about the disciples carrying the pizza boxes to the table and putting their arms around the newcomers. One class passing along the support they received coming in to the next.

That's all of it right there in a nutshell. Somebody reaches a hand out to you, and one day you reach out to take somebody else's.

And all of a sudden I think of Jordan.

One day when we were on our way from one place to another, he said to me, "I'd like to go on doing this with you for as long as I can."

Something clicks inside me. Not in my head, but right in my heart.

How's that feel?

"I feel like my mother's looking down from heaven and smiling," I say. "Me, a minister, and now my son accepting Jesus into his life."

Tracy moves her foot a little to the side so she can get a better look at my face.

"Passing the torch," she says.

"You got it," I say.

We put the bottoms of our feet back together and wait for the deer to show. It takes a little while, but then they're there.

The mother pokes her head out of the trees first, then the fawn behind her. They move together toward the house, stopping to snack on some grass along the way.

We stay quiet and we watch.

Chapter Eleven

The Circle

"Can the circle be unbroken
By and by Lord, by and by."
—"Can the Circle Be Unbroken," by Ada R. Habershon and Charles H. Gabriel, reworked by A.P. Carter

In August 2025, I get to celebrate a historic baseball moment that means a whole lot to Mets fans and me. Then, in September, I find myself standing to say goodbye to a man who helped shape both my life and the team's legacy.

Give life a chance and it'll close the circle of faith and purpose in ways you might never expect.

The setup for the moment is on Saturday, August 9, when Pete Alonso hits his 252nd home run against the Milwaukee Brewers, leading off the second inning at their home stadium and thumping a high fastball thrown by Brewers starter Tobias Myers over four hundred feet through the air. His shot ties the franchise home run record I held for thirty-seven years.

Three days later in the third inning of a game against the Braves at Citi Field in Queens, Pete hits number 253 against a pitcher named Spencer Strider. The ball flies 387 feet to the opposite field, just enough to get it over the wall in right-center.

That one breaks my record. Pete's second blast of the night, in the sixth, is icing.

The crowd gets loud, showing their appreciation.

When I broke the Mets home run record back in 1988, I didn't even realize it. I was focused on winning, not putting up numbers. Plus, the Mets were still a young franchise—only twenty-six years old compared to almost a century for teams like the Yankees and Cardinals—so the record held by Dave Kingman didn't feel like that big of a milestone.

Pete's homer is different. The team's become a regular postseason contender, with a roaring fan base, and I'd been part of their first real wave of success, helping to drive them to a World Championship. Kingman was a swing-for-the-fences power hitter. He wasn't homegrown, and he played during the team's down years. The farm system has developed other very talented players after me, but my record has stuck for all those decades.

It was way back in spring training that I told Steve Gelbs I was rooting for Pete. I said records are meant to be broken, and if anyone was going to do it, I was glad it was one of our own kids like him, who came up through the system.

The fans have a special connection to those players, and Pete's a standout talent. He has tremendous raw power. He doesn't have to pull the baseball, and can hit it to all fields. That's what makes him dangerous. When I played, they talked about my swing being easy, how the ball jumped. It's the same with Pete. The ball jumps off his bat. You don't see that too often.

People sometimes think you get to the big leagues and it's all success. But everybody has struggles. Pete's had his share, and he'll tell you that. But he never quit. He fought. That's what I love—the fight. He's shown that from day one.

I was at Citi Field for a game on August 7, hoping he'd hit the record-tying homer while I was in town (I came to New York for my grandson Jaylin's baptism—unlike his dad, Jordan, he wasn't going to wait till he reached his thirties!). But it didn't happen, and I watched it on television two days later like thousands of other Mets fans.

Why was I happy to see it?

A record only has meaning because it sets a bar later generations can reach for. It inspires them to learn their craft and accomplish great things. If it just sits there like some dusty old trophy on a high shelf, people forget about it, or maybe a commentator pulls it down from that shelf once in a blue moon. Like everything else in competitive sports, it's the athletes chasing after it who grab our attention.

My career's over. I had my success. I put my numbers up, and they stood a long time. Former players need to applaud the current ones who achieve great things. We need to cheer them on. Be a backbone for them.

There's nothing like the passion of New York fans. And when they speak, they speak loud. If you don't listen—if you can't hear what they're saying when you're not performing—then you need to have your ears checked.

When you run out there on the field, you want to be the best player you can be. To have people scream and cheer for you when you come through—at Shea we had almost *sixty thousand* when the house was full—and let you know when you stink, is what motivates some players. It definitely spurred *me* on. You want to hear them, and you want to win for them. But not all players can deal with it.

In New York, you've got to believe, and perform. You've got to stay in the fire of it. If not, the city will run you out. But if you stick through the storms, you get to stand tall.

Pete has done that. He's done a great job keeping himself healthy, staying consistent, and not listening to the media noise. He's showing people what he's made of. And now he's the Mets' Home Run King. He deserves all the praise he's getting for breaking the record.

The pregame ceremony honoring Pete is scheduled to take place August 13 at Citi Field, keeping it in the Mets' series against the Braves. I'm flooded with interview requests—television, radio, print, you name it. The Mets also ask me to do voice-over for a special video they're going to play on the 'tron.

I fly to New York after a few days at home with Tracy, wanting to congratulate Pete in person. I make sure to check into my hotel early that morning, so I can handle as many interview requests as possible from my room, and then head over to Citi for the celebration.

But that ends up getting postponed. It's one of those soggy days in New York when it rains on and off and they can't predict exactly when the game will start, so the team announces that Pete's celebration will be moved to the next day, August 14. That puts a hitch in my plans, because I have a major fundraiser for cancer treatment and research in Los Angeles—and I wouldn't miss that for anything. In 2020, twenty-five years after cancer took my mother, my sister Regina died of the disease. I go every year to honor them by helping out.

I spend the day doing interviews and preparing my video for the Mets. Pete has an opt-out in his contract after the season ends, and the TV and radio hosts all want to know whether I think he'll stay with the Mets or test the free agent market. But I can't really predict what will happen or give advice. It's up to him. He's got to ask himself: Do I stick and stay and make history here? He's already made it by breaking my record, of course. But he could play four, five more years and leave a real legacy of winning.

The records and numbers are great. But a championship with the Mets? That would mean everything. Pete talks about that all the time, and speaks about it during his ceremony.

I find it refreshing. That's what baseball, and playing in New York, is all about. Being able to leave a legacy, to put your stamp on it and say, "I came here, it was hard, but I stood up to it."

I also know what it's like to face that kind of decision. It's never just about money. Pete stayed. I left. At the time, I felt the Mets were heading down a losing course. Now it couldn't have better ownership. Steven and Alex Cohen are fans, first and foremost. They're down-to-earth, easy to communicate with, and they give the players everything they need to succeed.

That's one big difference in how things are run these days. But you make the best decision you can with what you've got in front of you. There's something about having one home. I never had that after I left. So for Pete? The opportunity to be a New Yorker for life? That's enormous. But I'm sure Pete has his own things to weigh. And it's up to him to make his own decision.

Not long after, he makes his choice, and it's to move on.

On one of the talk shows, the hosts ask me about a ball Pete signed for a fan: "Down goes Straw." They want to know what I think about it, if I feel it's an issue. I'm fine with the question, that's just how the wheel spins in the Big Apple, and there's also been some fuss on social media. But the truth is, I really don't think about it until they ask. And when they do, it doesn't bother me at all.

I'm a minister of the Gospel now, and that's where my heart is. That's the work that lasts. I think about spending time with men on Death Row. I think about visiting recovery centers, where people are trying to climb out of addiction. I think about people who are hurting, and need someone to pray for them and guide them forward.

Baseball will always be part of my story, and I'll always love it. But it's not my calling. It's not what defines me anymore.

A few weeks after Pete breaks the record, I get an unexpected call that drives this home.

I knew for a while that my former Mets skipper, Davey Johnson, had been in bad health. When he couldn't attend my jersey retirement the year before, it was a sure sign he wasn't doing well. On September 5, Davey's wife, Susan, tells Jay Horwitz that he's passed, and Jay makes the news public.

A day or two later, Susan reaches out to me with a text saying she wants me to be the main speaker at his funeral service.

My heart starts racing in my chest as I read it. Then I take a deep breath and answer that I'd be honored. It will mean canceling a preaching engagement at the last minute, and also flying from New York early after the Mets Alumni Classic game at Citi Field, an event Jay Horwitz put together. Though I don't intend to put on the full uniform for the game—that was a different life, and the uni stays off—I'll wear the jersey and meet the fans.

As it sinks in that I'll be delivering Davey's eulogy, I have a deep sense that God is once again working His will in ways we don't always see coming.

Davey Johnson was my manager when I was twenty-two. More than anyone else at the time, he helped me become a great player, and mature into a man. Because *he* was a great player, great leader, and great man.

Now, at sixty-three, the man I've become through Jesus Christ will have a chance, in some small way, to repay him.

Jordan and I land in Tampa, pick up Mead Chasky, and head down to Sarasota, where Davey's memorial service is being held. Mead has known him almost as long as I have, and when he heard he'd passed, he wanted to pay his respects.

The drive is about an hour and a half, and even Mead's on the quiet side today. I use the time behind the wheel to go over what I've been preparing since I heard from Susan.

As a friend and former player, I want to honor the life Davey shared with us by reflecting on the memories that defined him to me. I want to speak to who Davey was to the people who loved him, and who he still is in the Lord's presence, after spending eighty-two years in this world.

That's as a friend.

As a minister, I never give cookie-cutter sermons, and don't speak at memorial services unless I know the person and can talk about them from my heart. And I knew Davey well during one of the biggest times in both our lives.

But now I've been called to do something more. I'm sending Davey Johnson's immortal soul home to God, and that goes deeper than memories. It's not only about what I say. It's what God says.

The question we all have to ask ourselves while we're here is, "What's God going to say about me? About how I live my life, and what I do with the time I'm given?"

So, as I make my way down I-75 South, I think about what God might say about Davey, and pray I can be His vessel to say it right. I also make myself a promise: *This is not going to be a sad moment. I'm not about to cry. I'm gonna speak about a man whose life we're going to celebrate.*

By the time I get to Sarasota, I'm ready.

The church is a simple community place, white and modern-looking, palm trees all around, oaks with moss as we pull up front. You know you're in Florida when you see it.

Davey's family has hung the walls inside with framed jerseys, photos, and signed sports mementos. He had an All-Star playing career as an infielder with five teams, and managed four teams besides the Mets. He also loved his hockey, and there's a display with dozens of players he liked, all signed underneath.

It touches me to find my Mets jersey, with the 18 in back, hanging next to his number 5.

There are a few players in the church with Davey's family and non-baseball friends. Dave Magadan and Raffy Santana from our championship team, and Terry Leach, who was mostly up from the minors later on. There's also Bill Madden, the sportswriter, and Ron Goldstein, an attorney for the Yankees. It's a small group of baseball friends, but that's okay. It isn't about the number of people in the chapel—it's about the love inside it.

I think a lot of our players don't see the gift we were all given in that window of time. It was Davey who gave us a chance to be great. He was the gift, and he should be cherished.

Davey led us from nowhere to somewhere, from the bottom to the top, and turned the New York Mutts into the Mets. In 1983, my first year in the league, our record was 68 wins to 94 losses. A year later, when Davey became our manager, it was 90–72. In '85, we won 98 games. The next season, when we beat the Red Sox in the World Series, we won 108 regular season games.

But today's about much more than baseball.

Susan talks about her David—everyone outside the game called him David, she says—as a father, stepfather, and grandfather. He never took what happened on the field home with him. He loved his numbers, flying planes, and selling real estate. He bought his first property in 1960, and it became a passion that never let up. He played scratch golf when he could get to the course. He also really loved being a dad.

Davey wasn't a religious man in his younger years. But thanks to Susan, David came to know Jesus as sickness took over his body. She would read him Scripture, and then they'd read it together.

That brings me back. Davey and I would talk on the phone every so often, and I remember him saying, "Susan is doing great work with the church . . . just like you, Preacher Man." I think he got a kick out of calling me that, considering the crazy young guy he knew.

Susan shares a story that captures him perfectly. A few years ago, David was in a parking lot in his new Ford Explorer and got hit by another car. He called Susan to let her know.

"Are you all right?" she asked.

He told her he was fine and that the SUV was in good enough shape to drive. "But the guy who hit me could hardly speak English and didn't have any insurance," he said. "He was also an illegal immigrant."

"So what did you do?" Susan asked.

"I reached into my wallet, handed the guy a twenty, and told him to get the hell out of here as fast as he could," Davey told her.

That's pure Davey.

When Susan finishes, the pastor talks about Davey growing into his faith, and we sing one of the old hymns. It lifts every last one of us before I step up to take my turn at the pulpit.

Susan spoke for his family, and I start out speaking for the players. We knew him as our skipper. We knew him as our manager. We knew him as our leader, someone we could trust, someone who believed in all of us.

I go back to when I was twenty-one years old, in Tidewater, Triple-A, 1983. It's early May, probably the third week of the season, and I was hitting .333 with three home runs.

I don't need Davey's Einstein brain to know that amounts to a homer a week. But one day I get to the ballpark and notice I'm not in the lineup.

"What's up, Davey?" I said. "Why aren't I playing today?"

He says, "Come into my office."

Once we're inside, he closes the door, tells me to sit down, and I wait. I'm thinking something's definitely wrong. But I can't figure out what it might be. I hadn't done anything to get into trouble, at least as far as I knew. First week of May . . . I hardly had enough time for that!

Then he says, "You're going to the big leagues."

It was an overwhelming moment. If anything, I'd figured I had a chance of being called up later in the season. That's usually how it went.

My mouth must have dropped open. I started to say something—I don't know what—but all I could manage at first was, "Oh."

Davey put his hand out like a traffic cop and stopped me. "Don't do that," he says. "You're ready." And then he says, "I hope to see you one day soon."

He knew exactly what to say to get me ready for my journey. It wasn't a lot of words. But it didn't need to be. What matters isn't how many—just whether they're the right ones. And Davey knew how to do that.

He turned out to be right about seeing me again soon too. The very next year, 1984, Davey was promoted to manager of the New York Mets. He'd led the Tides to a championship, and the front office was hoping he could work the same magic with the Major League club.

They got their wish.

"When Davey took over, we became something else," I tell everyone. "He knew what every player needed to succeed. He knew every player's strengths and weaknesses. Davey was analytics before there were analytics. He was like a computer, a wizard at operating between the lines and controlling the game."

But it didn't end there. Because Davey had been a player and understood how hard it could be, he wasn't going to let the front office rule over us. He stood up for his guys. He protected us. In a baseball town like New York, that meant everything. We became a team of destiny. Personality. Swagger. Toughness. Davey gave everyone in our clubhouse the same feeling of confidence he gave me that day I was promoted to the majors.

We were the wildest team you could ever imagine, but he didn't care—he loved us anyway. If you didn't show up on time, he'd fine you. He fined me plenty of times. "That's $500," he'd say. And then he'd tell you, "I still love you."

Like I said a minute ago, that was Davey.

I think the first time he slapped me with a fine was when I missed a Sunday workout at spring training. Another was in Chicago, when I went into the clubhouse in the ninth inning of a blowout loss, when I should've stayed in the dugout until the end of the game. It got so hot between us, Ron Darling had to step in the middle to stop it from coming to blows.

Davey was in the right both times, and I knew it, so I figured I deserved to pay up. The truth is, I was young and stubborn, and I thought five hundred was a small price to pay.

Once, he got mad about something and fined me three thousand dollars. Probably he figured that much money would sting enough for me to fall in line.

I told Davey, "*Three thousand!*"

He just shrugged. "Don't worry," he said. "I'll donate it to charity. And don't forget I love you."

The Mets of that era were like the bad boys in *Animal House*. I'd never want to deny it or go back and change anything, because all our rowdiness and nightclubbing off the field made us a tighter group on it. Whatever people said or wrote about us only made us pull closer together, and Davey gave us room to be ourselves. He was his own man, and he allowed us to be the same way. He let us be the animals in *Animal House*. All he asked in return was that we show up and play hard, with the goal of bringing home a championship.

"We came so close in '85," I say at the service. "I remember our last home game, when we looked up at the scoreboard and saw the Cardinals had clinched the National League East. We won ninety-eight games, but they won three more, and we didn't make the playoffs."

Our locker room was quiet. Just . . . quiet. The air felt heavy, like it was pressing down on us. That feeling sat in us the whole offseason.

"Then we came to spring training in 1986," I remember. "Davey was like a general. He said, 'We're gonna win it all.' Not 'We're going to try.' We're going to win. And then he used a word I'll never forget. He said, 'We're going to *dominate*.'"

I know the media didn't buy it. And when we got off to a 2–3 start, and the newspaper writers got on us, it made the fans have their doubts.

But Davey didn't second-guess himself. Or, if he did, he didn't show us. He got us to believe.

He taught us not to quit. To never give up no matter the circumstances. And though I didn't realize it at the time, it's crystal clear now he wasn't just teaching us about baseball. Everything he taught us could be applied to life.

"We are the Mets," he'd say. "We are New York. The other teams are gonna hate you, so you better show up for every game."

I recall him telling me I was the kind of player who could carry the team for a month. "Everybody can't do that," he said. But he believed I could. And when someone like Davey believes in you, it changes everything.

We did exactly what he said. We dominated. Our team won 108 regular-season games, went to the World Series, and beat the Red Sox in seven games.

That's why it hit our core group so hard when he got fired in 1990.

We were off to a slow start, and the front office didn't like how Davey handled things. He didn't blame the players in the media. He didn't throw us under the bus. He kept letting us be who we were, like he'd done all along during the winning years.

But the people upstairs wanted something different. They wanted a quieter clubhouse, one that was more buttoned-up.

They wanted milk drinkers. Davey's attitude was, "These are my guys. They can drink whatever they want."

It was a difficult time for us. And not long after Davey left, I left for Los Angeles.

Now I look out at everybody in front of me, the people who loved Davey Johnson the most. There's still one baseball story left to tell of the dozens in my head. It's short, but important.

In 1996, Davey and I had both moved on from the Mets. Our championship year was a decade behind us, and he was managing the Baltimore Orioles. I was with the Yankees after George Steinbrenner, the Boss, personally asked me to sign in spite of my struggles with addiction. He took a chance on me, and said something like, "I know all about Daryl's problems. But he's a young man who was important to baseball at one point, and I wonder whether he can be important again."

My first year in the Bronx, wouldn't you know it, we went up against Davey's Baltimore team and beat them in the ALCS. It was a crushing loss for his team.

When the last game ended, Davey came over to our clubhouse and found me.

That's rarer than rare, a manager showing up in the opposing clubhouse after a playoff loss, while the champagne's spraying and the team's whooping and hollering. I honestly don't know if it ever happened before or since.

Davey came. He walked right up to me, gave me a big hug, told me how proud he was of me. And then he told me he loved me.

A word they use a lot to describe certain kinds of relationships nowadays is "transactional." It means someone says he loves you because he needs something from you, because there's something to gain.

There was nothing transactional about Davey walking into our clubhouse on our home turf, in the middle of our celebration, even though he was hurting for himself and his guys.

But that's who he was. A father figure. A mentor.

I tell everyone at the memorial service that knowing him, playing under him, learning from him was a joy. That's me speaking as a former ballplayer.

But I haven't been a ballplayer for a very long time. I'm a minister now, a preacher. Davey helped me take the biggest step in my baseball career. Now it's my turn to help him take the next step that we all have to take, the journey that comes after this life is over.

I look at Susan from the pulpit and quote one of my favorite psalms from the Bible, Psalm 30:5: "Weeping may endure for a night, but joy comes in the morning." I want her to know I didn't come here to shed tears. I loved her David.

I came to celebrate him.

"Thank you for leading him to the right person," I say to her. "There's nobody greater than Jesus. We can achieve all these great things, fame and fortune, but at the end of the day, it's the Lord Jesus that we need to lead people to. And you've done that. You've been a wonderful wife, a wonderful lady for him. So thank you. God is well pleased with you."

I believe when God greeted Davey, He would have said, "Well done, My good and faithful servant." Like all of us, Davey had his trials and tribulations. But he was good to people. And he did good on this earth. Sometimes, in the middle of our loss, it's hard to see that absence from the body means being present with the Lord. I remind everyone of it, so they can know with confidence that Davey Johnson's present with God.

It's as I finish my eulogy and get ready to lead the group in prayer that I remember the last time I saw him. Mead set it up with Susan a few months ago, after telling me Davey wasn't doing well. They both lived in Florida, and it was typical for Mead to show up at his door for a visit.

But no one told Davey I was coming. I can see it like it's happening right now.

We drive over, and I wait outside his house. When Susan tells him Mead's dropped by, he comes through the door, spots me, and freezes for a second like he can't believe his eyes. Then he walks right over with his arms out for a big hug.

"What's up, Davey!" I say. We're all smiles. "The *great* Davey Johnson!"

He's still hugging me. "How's The Preacher doing?"

Our smiles get even bigger.

"Davey, can you believe I'm a preacher, as crazy as I was?"

He goes, "No, I cannot believe it."

But it's all over his face that he can. He looks proud. And I know it isn't what I did as a ballplayer—it's who I've become as a man.

"How you doing, man?" I ask, putting my arm around him. He's so thin, I can feel every bone.

"Good," he says, and we make a little small talk. He asks where I'm living. I ask how old he is now.

"Eighty-two." For a numbers wizard, he says it like that one doesn't add up.

"Bless your heart," I say. "You're the greatest manager I ever played for."

Mead's got his phone out, and I pull Davey close against my side.

"This guy right here," I say, pointing into the camera. "He was great. Y'all just don't know."

Standing there with him that afternoon, Mead holding up that phone, I never would've guessed I'd be here today. Leading the people who loved him most in prayer. Speaking over his life. Sending him home.

But God had His plan. God always has a plan.

It's like everything I was, and everything I've become, have come together in this moment.

I bow my head, grateful for the man Davey was, the love in this room, and the chance to honor him in the best way I know how.

I used to play for him. Today, I get to pray for him.

"Father, thank You for this time. Thank You for his family. Father, I ask that You comfort them in this difficult time. Father . . ."

We've come full circle, and I know that would make Davey proud.

I'm on a plane from New York to Chicago, my bags packed for over two weeks on the road. After Chicago, I have a speaking engagement in North Carolina for a group that brings Bible study to people behind bars, a ministry trip with Tracy to Tennessee (we're meeting up in Atlanta), and a pair of men's events in Utica and Syracuse, New York. There's a couple of baseball-related appearances in between.

I've been on the move since Davey's funeral. After his service a few days ago, I flew back to New York just long enough to speak at last night's fundraiser for the Fred L. Mazzilli Foundation.

Lee Mazzilli, my old Mets teammate, and his wife run it in honor of his brother, who died of lung cancer because it didn't get caught in time. I was given an award, but what mattered more to me was getting to speak about what it means to fight through cancer and keep going. The foundation helps with early screenings in underserved neighborhoods like Coney Island, where smoking rates are high and access to care is low. I've mentioned that I saw cancer take my mom and sister, and Tracy's walked through it in her own steady, quiet way. So that part's always personal.

This morning, I hurried to LaGuardia Airport and caught an early flight out to O'Hare. With two hours in the air ahead of me, I've been mostly thinking about life coming full circle, like I started doing at the funeral service—about how things connect, break, and come back around according to God's plan.

That'll happen whether or not you accept your place in it. But God will always remind you of who He's called you to be. When you're willing to pay attention and understand your purpose, things come around in a way that can transform you and everything around you.

There's an old Gospel song called "Can the Circle Be Unbroken." Most of us know it, even if we can't remember all the words or if we first heard it in church or on the radio. But the meaning sticks with you. It's about a mother passing on from this life, and the singer talking about the family's pain but knowing she's with God. Then the singer asks if the family will ever be whole again.

I know that happens, know it to be true. God really does bring things full circle. The only word I can use for it is one I use all the time: *miraculous.*

I think about Angola Prison, and the story of Eugene Tanniehill. He was young, using dope, and killed a minister. Years later, he became the first pastor ever ordained at Angola. If that's not full circle, I don't know what is.

I think about James in hospice care, the inmate who got me mixed up with Eric Dickerson and his prescription goggles, and then Tracy asking to see the photo of me praying with him next to the one of me and my dying father. I fought Tracy tooth and nail before going to see Dad. But the grace of forgiveness I gave and received that day is what clinched me becoming a true minister of the Gospel. Could I have led James to the Lord if my heart had never been released from its own prison? I'm pretty sure the answer's no. The Lord reminds you of the work He assigns you to do for His Kingdom in all kinds of ways.

I think about Saugerties, Carole and Vince Kelder using the loss of their son to rescue other young people from addiction. I was in my hotel room there when I remembered Gene Dusan and Big Mac helping me get past the racism in Lynchburg, and then decided to use that memory when I spoke to those kids on the baseball team about relying on each other.

Now I'm thirty thousand feet up, flying west across the country, but my mind keeps moving through the circle He's laid out for me. The Lord has a plan for each of us. If you open your eyes and your heart, it can't be missed.

I remember Gary Carter saying God was going to use me mightily. I remember my mother's prediction. *You're going to go through it. But He's going to get it out of you.* I think about Jordan traveling with me over the past two years, fathering a child, getting baptized. I don't know what future he'll choose. He may not even know it yet. But wherever his path leads, I've done my best as his dad to help prepare him for it.

Pete Alonso breaking my home run record, now on his own path with the Orioles. That day my number went up at Citi Field—my family, friends, and teammates all there, the pastors I invited—that was when my legacy as a player became unbroken from my legacy as a preacher.

I nearly didn't make it there. The heart attack three months before could have killed me. Until then, I never really thought about my own mortality. I took it for granted that I'd have plenty of time—time to do my Kingdom work, time to finish the assignment God's given me, time to see my family grow. Part of me still hadn't matured past the ballplayer who thought he was invulnerable.

There's a line from Ecclesiastes: "For everything there is a season, and a time for every purpose under heaven." I'd bet whoever wrote the hymn I was thinking of knew it really well.

Everyone has a season, and every season ends and comes 'round again. Some seasons end in loss, but God always brings renewal. I don't know when my final season will come, but realizing that as I was wheeled into surgery taught me not to take one single moment of it for granted.

It taught me to use every one of these moments to become a better man and husband. It taught me to refocus on the work God's called me to.

As a friend, a player, and a minister, I just celebrated a life well lived—saying goodbye to Davey Johnson, the ending of his season in this world.

But as a proud pop and a man, I'm flying out to a new beginning in Chicago. A whole new season.

My daughter Jade is getting married the day after tomorrow, and I'm heading there to give her away.

You *know* it's always Dad who gets the first dance.

Epilogue

Isn't She Lovely?

My daughter picked the song, and it's as perfect as our moment. Just her and me, Jade and Dad having that first dance. I didn't know what it would be—my travel schedule didn't give us time to rehearse—and that's okay. We're winging it to Stevie's "Isn't She Lovely," a song he wrote about his little girl, like I used to call Jade, who isn't so little anymore.

She's 5'11", tall enough to throw her arms around my neck, and I can't pick her up and swing her around like before. Those Strawberry genes strike again.

I'm wearing a black shirt and black pants, sharp and simple, designer sneakers for my battered baseball player's feet. Jade's the princess in lace, a long white dress with a flowing skirt that reaches the floor. It's a fairy-tale room, crystal lights, candles, red roses hanging from the ceiling, a black-and-white checkerboard floor like you'd see in an old grand hotel.

I catch Tracy's eyes and feel the steady love she's always shown me and all of us, all her kids, even though she's not Jade's mom by birth. Charisse, Jade's mother, sharing our moment with grace and warmth. Kevin, my new son-in-law, smiling from the table.

All of us, our big, blended family, here to cherish this day.

We hold hands, step together on the floor. Stevie's singing that line about not believing what God has done, and it's just so incredible, so right for this dance. We make faces at each other, ham it up, shaking our heads the same way like we're looking in a goofy mirror. The happiness on Jade's face feels like warm sunshine on mine—or maybe it's the other way around since I'm beaming with joy.

They say a good ballplayer needs to be able to dance, and between Jade's time on the college volleyball court and my years on the field, father and daughter, we've both still got the fancy footwork. She leans back and sways; I catch her. She spins, and Dad manages to keep up without letting go of her hand.

Our dance is a gift. After everything—the pain, mistakes, the long road from where I was to where I am—I know I've been given a reward that's greater than anything I ever imagined possible. No record, no trophy, no fame or fortune could ever compare. And it's all from Him, a wonderful testament that His hand has been guiding my life all along.

When life knocks you down, His grace can rebuild you in ways you never imagined.

I can almost see Mama looking down on us. She'd be beaming just like her youngest son, knowing he's finally found his way, and that the torch of love, faith, and family is being passed on. It's an answer to every prayer she had for me, and all of us, back in Crenshaw, and every prayer I whispered when I was lost and broken.

And here I am now. This moment, the first dance with my daughter, is something I wouldn't trade for anything. But Kevin's waiting patiently for the next dance, and I'm not going to hog his beautiful bride.

I step aside, happy for both of them, feeling the renewal this brings deep in my heart.

It's a passing of the torch from what was to what will be. From the broken person I once was when I was younger to the man I'm still becoming.

From a lifetime of lessons learned in the dugout and the church to the work God's called me to now.

A passing of the torch and a reminder that, no matter the season, and whether there's sunshine or stormy weather, that light keeps moving forward.

I'll keep carrying it, wherever God leads me next.

A Note of Gratitude

It always happens. Reach for the phone, and the ringing stops before you pick up. Don't reach, and it rings twenty-nine times before finally leaving you alone.

I was sleeping hard on the couch. I didn't want to answer the phone. I didn't want to hear it. But it wouldn't quit.

I figured, wait. I can outlast it. I'm the boss. Plus, I'm more doggone tired than it is noisy. And like I've said before, I can be stubborn.

I was home helping Tracy recover from major back-to-back surgeries in November 2025, a few weeks after delivering this book to the publisher. It had been one of the hardest and best weeks of my life—hardest because I hated seeing her weak and in pain, best because I loved taking care of her. There are different ways of being exhausted. This was the good way.

It was a treat bringing Trace back from the hospital and making her as stable and comfortable as possible. But it was very challenging for us, because she was always in discomfort. She couldn't move around much and just getting up and down was an ordeal, so she stayed on the couch most of the day.

I wasn't scheduling any preaching or charitable engagements, letting me be a husband and care for her round-the-clock—helping her eat when she could hardly lift a fork to her mouth, making sure she took her medication when she was supposed to, washing the dishes, doing the laundry. It was a warm feeling, and a special experience, because I was used to being on the receiving end. She'd done the same for me so often in my life, I couldn't even begin to count the times. It was time for me to step up.

God always gives us chances to find opportunities inside the hardships we face. It's like breaking open a rock and finding beautiful crystals inside. We would sit in the living room for hours, me in a chair, Trace on the couch, and we'd talk, and sometimes cry together. I would encourage her when she felt bad, or was in serious pain, reminding her she'd get better. It might take a little while, but she was going to get well.

The second surgery was the roughest thing. I'd gone on the road for a few days to honor commitments from months before, ministerial work for organizations we couldn't let down. Some of the kids were over to help when Tracy started having terrible cramps. The doctor recommended she come in for a CT, and found complications from the first operation that required an emergency procedure.

I was in shock when Jesse, our pastor, called me to explain what was happening. There I was thousands of miles away, devastated. I remember bawling away in my hotel room. All I wanted was to be with my wife.

I remember Pastor Jesse saying, "The doctor knows exactly what he has to do. He came out and explained everything but needs to talk with you."

Then he took the phone and gave me the details. He told me he didn't want to wait.

I asked, "What would you do if it was your wife?"

When he said he would take her into surgery right away, I gave my consent.

The operation lasted two hours. Trace got out around midnight. My family called and said she's good, she's in recovery now, but I didn't sleep a wink that night.

I attended the fundraiser I'd come for, and with the Lord's help, I fulfilled my purpose. Then I drove home right afterward, crossing two state lines.

When I got back to Missouri, Tracy had been moved to a hospital room. I drove there without stopping at the house, pulled into the lot, and went straight up.

She saw me come in and we both burst into tears.

Within two seconds we were hugging on the bed. I cried so hard, told her I was so sorry she had to go through this, and promised I wouldn't leave her side again. I'd taken care of our ministry's obligations, and now only had to take care of her.

I'll never forget the look in her eyes when she said, "I know you will."

If you ever wondered if it's possible to be weeping away and thinking, *This is the coolest thing in the world* at the same time, I can tell you for a fact that it is.

After a few days, Tracy finally got out and came home again. I was back to taking care of her.

To everyone reading this, men and women—but maybe especially the men—I want to say there's nothing like it. There's nothing more rewarding, no greater gift, than being available for the ones you love when they're in their greatest need. And part of that gift, all wrapped up with it, is the realization of what it would be like to lose that person.

I remember thinking: If Trace is down, I need to be up for her. I'll run out of the house to get whatever groceries she wants, whatever kind of fruit (she likes fruit!), whatever she needs. I was glad to do it. It was never a burden. It put no pressure on me. I wanted her to get well. And that's all I wanted.

Too often we miss out on the joy of caring for someone we love because we're busy thinking about everything else we have to do. We don't take time to put stuff aside. I'm grateful because we were getting toward the end of the year, when my traveling on behalf of our ministry slows down.

Looking back, I truly believe God arranged the timing. He knew Tracy would have to go through what she was going through, and wanted me home to take care of her.

Along with my service to Him, she is my whole life.

And right about now, I bet you're wondering how my ringing phone fits into everything I just wrote.

Well, it all comes together in one word: gratitude.

When the ringing started, I was stretched out on the couch in the family room around 4:30 PM. Tracy was in the living room, lying on the couch there. I'd been sleeping for a while, a deep sleep after a full day of chores and errands, and I was, like, *Phone, go away.*

I finally cracked open an eye and looked over to see who was calling. The screen had a 202 area code, and I knew that was Washington, DC.

I didn't recognize the number. I usually don't answer numbers I don't know. And I couldn't think of anyone I knew in DC. But I was curious.

Let me answer. This might be Larry.

Larry's a friend who works with the Trump organization on the golf side of things, which is how we got to know each other. I didn't figure he'd be calling from the capital. But no one else came to mind.

I picked up the phone and heard a young woman's voice.

"Mr. Strawberry," she said, "you have a call from the president of the United States, Donald J. Trump."

Holy smoke, I thought. All of a sudden, I was wide awake. I mean, a call from the president—that's enough to get anybody up off the couch.

I ran into the living room with Tracy and put the phone on speaker. The next thing I knew, the president came on the line.

I've known President Trump for a long time, dating back to my days playing in New York. He was always gracious to me, even during my short period on *Celebrity Apprentice*. And he was just as gracious on the phone. He talked about loving baseball and remembered how I could run and hit when I was with the Mets and Yankees in the 1980s and '90s. I joked about him being able to hit a golf ball, and he laughed and said he was never that good.

Then he said, "I just want to let you know I'm gonna give you a clean record. You had some problems. But you've done so much good work, and you've helped so many other people, you deserve to be pardoned."

Mistakes. I knew he meant the run-ins with drugs and financial mistakes that ended with me serving jail time in the early 2000s.

So many things ran through my head. In both a real and spiritual sense, I'd been free for the last twenty years, doing the work of a minister. God hasn't held my past failings over my head but has opened doors for me to go anywhere to share His Word. I knew I was not a felon in His eyes. In His eyes, I'd been redeemed long ago.

But I have to be straight—this was like icing on the cake He had already given me. At a barbecue in New York the summer before, Larry had brought up the idea of a pardon because of the transformation I'd undergone and my work with the ministry, but I hardly gave it any thought afterward.

The best thing about it? It wasn't about politics. It was about who I am and my focus on what I do in life. And it felt wonderful.

After a second, the president asked, "Where's your wife?"

I said, "She's right here, listening."

And he said, "Tracy, your husband is cleaner than you now."

We laughed. No way could that *ever* be true. But the word *clean* stuck with me.

I remember the president saying, "Live good lives for yourselves, be happy, and continue doing what you're doing," and Tracy thanking him for what he did for me. And that was it.

The call lasted about four minutes, start to finish, and when it ended,

I found myself overwhelmed with gratitude, praising God for helping me become a better man, husband, and father.

I'm free, I thought. *I'm free.*

Free, humbled, and thankful for this whole other life I've been given.

It's in that spirit that I invite you, my friends, to embrace gratitude for all God gives us, and to make the greatest use of it by helping others.

If you can take a little of that spirit from this book, I guarantee it will turn purpose into power, and make every life you touch better.

—Darryl Strawberry, 2026

Acknowledgments

To my Lord and Savior, Jesus Christ, who Saved me, healed me, and transformed me. All glory to You, forever.

My mother, Ruby Strawberry, who left the legacy of Christ for all of us kids.

My wife, Tracy—your prayers, fight, and love led me back to Jesus. I love you deeply and forever.

DJ, Diamond, Alice, Jordan, Omar, Austin, Evan, Jade, Jewel, and Michael: My last request in life is for my life's example in Christ to lead you into your own deep relationship with Him. Love you all so much.

Ma and Papa Leonard—you have been the constant love and example of Christ in my life. I love you.

Gerry and Peggy Boulware, my father- and mother-in-law who never gave up on me. I love you, Mom and Dad.

My siblings: Mike, Ronnie, Michelle, Regina—I couldn't ask for a better life with you. Love you guys.

The Mets organization: for honoring my achievements, retiring my number, and my life in faith.

Jay Horwitz, thank you for your friendship and raising me up in the Mets organization. I love you, Buddy.

Journey Church, and Pastor Jesse Quiroz, for your constant covering. You are my true Brother in Christ.

Leah Wilson and everyone at BenBella Books, along with Tom Hopke and Doug Grad, for believing in me and the message God put in me for this book.

Rick Chillot, our great editor at BenBella, for his attention and patience.

Jerome (Ronie), my writer and now Brother—you witnessed and wrote this beautiful masterpiece. Love you, Buddy. Suzanne, thanks for lending me your husband for all these many months.

To all my true friends who have walked this journey with me. You know who you are.

To all the churches, pastors, organizations, and servants of God—keep fighting the good fight of faith, loving, helping, and leading the broken and lost.

About the Authors

Darryl Strawberry

With four World Series rings, baseball legend Darryl Strawberry is one of the greatest hitters in the long history of the New York Mets and held the team's home run record for thirty-seven years. He ranks among the top twenty on the *New York Times* list of New York City's one hundred most famous (and favorite) people. Yet Darryl's success on the field came hand in hand with personal struggles, including substance abuse, divorces, cancer, and jail time.

Some twenty years ago, he overcame the demons of his childhood trauma through Jesus Christ and found true redemption and restoration. Today, as an ordained minister of the Gospel, his purpose and passion are to help others transform their lives.

Darryl travels the country 270 days a year, sharing his message of hope and restoration with people from all walks of life. Among those who benefit from his work are families in crisis, patients in children's hospitals, young athletes, individuals in recovery, prison inmates, and residents of homes for troubled youths.

He is the author of the *New York Times* bestseller *Straw: Finding My Way* (2009) and 2021's *Turn Your Season Around: How God Transforms Your Life*.

Darryl lives in the St. Louis area with his wife, Tracy.

Jerome Preisler

A multiple *New York Times* bestselling author of more than forty novels and works of nonfiction, Jerome Preisler is the coauthor of NBA Hall of Famer Bernard King's acclaimed 2018 memoir, *Game Face: A Lifetime of Hard-Earned Lessons On and Off the Basketball Court*.

Among Jerome's many works of narrative nonfiction is *Daniel's Music: One Family's Journey from Tragedy to Empowerment Through Faith, Medicine, and the Healing Power of Music*—the gripping story of an ordinary family who turn personal trials into a force that brings joy, inspiration, and a powerful sense of belonging to everyone whose lives they touch.

From 2005 to 2013, he wrote the baseball column "YankeesInk" for YESNetwork.com. Lauded for its focus on human-interest stories and coverage of the Yankees' HOPE Week, it quickly became one of the most visited pages on the site.

Jerome has been a frequent collaborator in the Tom Clancy franchise and recently oversaw and wrote the relaunch of the popular Net Force series.

A native of Brooklyn, he lives in New York City and Maine with his wife, Suzanne.